BEFORE THE COUCH

SIMPLE AND SURPRISING HELP FOR CHRISTIAN COUPLES

DR. BILL SENYARD

Foreword by
SHARI Y. JOHANSSON

THE
GOSPEL
APP

For my wife and editor, Eunice, my family and for my God whose love for the unlovable, unloved, unlovely, unworthy and unlikely—like me —continues to surprise me day in and day out.

CONTENTS

FOREWORD

BY SHARI Y. JOHANSSON, MA, LPC, NCC,
BCN, QEEGD-DL

Before the Couch is a helpful guide for marriages. All marriages could benefit, but this is written especially for those in the truly tough seasons—for those who are exhausted and disillusioned. This book is both practical and ethereal, much like its author.

I met Bill Senyard in 2009 as part of the pastoral search committee for my church. He won my vote and my heart because, without prompting, he stated that the position and move to Colorado must be good for—and agreed upon with—his wife. Being a therapist who believes that a big part of my mission, and the mission of the church, is to uphold marriage and families, I knew he was the one who would bring this message to our community.

Bill has indeed been that pastor and advocate for marriages. *Before the Couch* brings his voice and wisdom to a wider audience.

In these pages, we see that marriage is more than a social construct or contract. Marriage is a sacred echo of a greater story. Dr. Senyard reminds us so insightfully that we are vessels with cracks—leaky and deeply in need of being filled before we can pour into our partners or our marriages.

Over three decades of counseling couples, I have seen how the cultural narratives around marriage—shaped by Hollywood and Disney—have warped our understanding and, therefore, our approach to marriage. The cultural idea has become akin to a quest for self-fulfillment. But marriage is a living parable of something far greater. That modern view is out of sync with God's purposes and leaves us empty.

This book affirms so clearly that we cannot give what we have not received. It is an invitation to abide. Marriage, in this light, becomes a crucible for ongoing growth and transformation.

Bill speaks with the wisdom of a shepherd and the candor of a fellow traveler. He says the quiet part out loud: "I can't do it." And into that honest admission, he speaks hope—not the fluffy kind, but hope rooted in God's miraculous power to love through us.

Our quest is to come to the end of ourselves so that we might rest in the truth that God is the author of our stories—and our marriages are part of the larger story that God is telling.

I know firsthand the transforming power of this truth, and I am excited to use this book as a guide for the couples I am privileged to walk alongside. It is a relief from the strife of trying harder.

There are practical exercises that are accessible and bring an element of fun to the process.

Most of all, this book does not pretend. It does not shame or overburden those who are hurt and empty. It points us to the only Source that does not run dry.

If you come to this book drained, I invite you to let yourself be filled. Let these pages guide you toward experiencing God's love and grace more deeply. And through the mystery of Christian marriage, let your relationship journey be restored.

BEFORE THE COUCH

Christian couples, I am for you. This book is for you. Jesus is surely for you. You have not messed that up. You can't. There is always hope!

Here's what you should know about *Before the Couch*.

- *Before The Couch* is a safe space, free from guilt and shame, allowing you to explore your relationship without fear or judgment.
- Your relational struggles are not *all* your or your partner's fault.
- Your relationship *is* redeemable, but that is not in your toolbox.
- What you've been doing hasn't worked, so STOP IT! Take a pause. Honestly, what you've been doing to try to fix your relationship has only exacerbated the problems.
- This book is not meant to replace counseling. You most likely need the professional couch. We all do at times. But *Before the Couch* is here to complement your counseling,

providing surprising and straightforward tips to make subsequent sessions far more effective.

- *Before The Couch* majors on the surprising Gospel of God's love for the unlovable, unlovely, and unloved. God loves relationship failures. That's all of us on any given day.

Remember, you are not alone in this journey. Couples, you've got this.

PRE-COUCH WARM-UP: JUST GETTING STARTED

"The deepest principle in human nature is the craving to be appreciated."

— WILLIAM JAMES

"Craving to be appreciated usually doesn't work."

— UNKNOWN

"Every child needs at least one adult
     who is irrationally crazy about him or her."

— URIE BRONFENBRENNER

THE CHRISTIAN COUPLE, visibly tense, entered my office and took their seats on opposite ends of the comfy couch. It didn't take a Dr. Phil to sense things were rocky.

"Hey, Sarah, Joe, I'm glad you're here. What's been on your

mind lately?" I asked, trying to sound hopeful. I was sure nothing I said would be helpful now—too much bad blood.

Sarah, the bold one, spoke up immediately with apparent frustration. "We did the love language survey you suggested, Pastor Bill. I thought it was very insightful. My love language is clearly *words of affirmation*. That's what I have been trying to tell Joe, even though he never listens."

"But babe, we've talked about this, I..." Joe tried to break in to defend himself.

"Joe, there you go again, interrupting me. You see what I mean, Pastor?"

Words of affirmation? Ironical, I thought to myself.

She continued, "I felt a little hopeful after the survey. Joe seemed to agree that my love language was affirmation. But nothing changed. I want Joe to step up and *love me the way I want to be loved. That's what I deserve. Am I right?* I guess he does other things. His love language is service, and he tries. *But it doesn't satisfy my need, my itch. That is not how God made me.* I have concluded we are just not compatible. Will you talk to him? I am at the end of my rope."

Perhaps you can relate to one or both partners. I could have told the exact same story with Joe as the prime spokesperson. It is not a male or female bent. It is a post-fall human phenomenon. You are not alone in this struggle.

At this stage of a rapidly declining relationship, it is normal and very human for both partners to have become self-focused and turned inward. "I want to be loved the way I want."

I prefer not to use the term *selfish* due to its harsh negative connotation, but this very human, reactionary programming is *anti-Jesus*.

Do nothing out of selfish ambition or vain conceit, but in humility consider others better than yourselves. Each of you should look not only to your own interests, but also to the interests of others. Your attitude should be the same as that of Christ Jesus.

— PHIL. 2:3-5

This *self-prioritizing bent* is not *all* our fault. Its genesis is in our brains' inner working models, some of which have been around since infancy. Our reactionary midbrain is entirely in charge, and our rational prefrontal cortex has been brilliantly bypassed or even chemically shut down by cortisol.

In one sense, our midbrain is working against our relationship. Though we believe we are being reasonable, we are not.

To be clear, we humans do not have the innate capacity to do Philippians 2—at least not the way that our partners long for and deserve—or Jesus desires.

❦

But here's the good news: while our love often bends toward self-interest—especially when strained by ongoing conflict—God's love is inherently and perfectly other-oriented. In fact, it's the only love that truly is.

Even better? His Spirit dwells within every believer, including those who are struggling in their relationships. The love that flows between the Father and the Son—the same love with which we are loved—is not beyond our reach.

Before the Couch will help you begin to *experience* and *express* that love, both personally and within your marriage.

In short, the approach of *Before the Couch* depends on something greater than human effort: it requires regular miracles—acts of God that alone can overcome our natural tendency toward reactionary self-centeredness.

In the chapters ahead, we'll explore how to stop taking ourselves so seriously, rediscover what love truly is, and, most importantly, what the love of God is.

How will this happen? By reversing the usual order. Rather than starting with ourselves, we take small, intentional steps to access the power of God through the Spirit in our inner being, allowing us to grasp the love of Christ—for both ourselves and our spouse (Eph. 3:14–21).

As we grow in our experience of God's love, both personally and relationally, our understanding of love is reshaped. As our souls are filled with the fullness of the Father (Eph. 3), we'll find that we naturally begin to take ourselves less seriously.

Welcome to *Before the Couch*.

2

TIP #1: STOP IT!

"Let's go Catherine. I am going to say two words to you right now. I want you to listen very carefully. I want you to take them out of the [counseling] office with you and to incorporate them into your life. You ready. Okay, here they are. "STOP IT. S.T.O.P—new word—I.T."

— BOB NEWHART-"STOP IT!"

COUPLES, aren't you tired of being told what you should be doing? You probably know and have tried most of those suggestions already. Am I right? And how's that going for you?

So, here's where we will begin. One surprising and simple tip that each of you can do before you even sit on the counselor's couch to discuss your relationship issues.

Stop what you are doing. It obviously isn't working. Truth be told, it likely isn't helping anyone. It's not all your fault. Don't worry about feeling like a failure.

Let me remind you, our God innately loves failures. That's all of us on any given day if we were just a little bit honest. Trust me, He is

5

not disappointed in you. In fact, He is pursuing you right now with an undiminished, furious love that should take your breath away. Your biggest problem is not your partner or your relationship. Something in your midbrain is blocking you from grasping the height, width, length, and depth of the love of Jesus for you right now.

No worries, there's hope. Sit back and enjoy the ride.

CASE STUDY

A few years ago, our congregation had a growing number of young couples, many of whom were struggling in their marriages. We organized a relationship weekend to provide some much-needed guidance and encouragement.

Friday evening finally came. The room was packed. Young couples were ready with laptops, and older couples were prepared with pens and paper pads. There were singles and single-again, divorcees, most of whom were caught up in the swirling, stressful currents of modern relationships.

There were the usual suspects as well, the issues and baggage that come alongside most relationships today: family of origin patterns, unresolved wounds and hurts, infidelity (actual or emotional), porn, fear that dark secrets might be exposed, physical and emotional abuse, brain inner-working models (the subconscious beliefs and thought patterns that were hardwired even as far back as infancy), addictions, fears of having married the wrong person. There were sexuality issues, loneliness, isolation, a lack of feelings of desire and desirability, guilt for not being a better partner after the last six marriage seminars attended—and, of course, shame and guilt related to their relationship with God.

"I know I am supposed to love my partner. I wonder if God is disappointed in me?"

Does any of that sound familiar?

Of course, no one was sharing these feelings aloud in the group

—not yet. Unfortunately, it just wasn't done. A truly safe place was required. That was our goal, but we hadn't quite reached it as a congregation.

After breaking the ice with a couple of humorous videos, we educated the group on recent marriage and divorce statistics, as well as some of the latest research on the leading causes of divorce.

Good news. While the divorce rate for first-time marriages remains between 40 and 50%, it declined by almost 30% between 2008 and 2023. Bad news. A disturbing rise (4.3%) has been noted since 2020—hopefully, this is not a trend.

I can remember when the two biggest reasons for divorce were #1 —finances and #2—infidelity. But today, the lists are dramatically different.

Surprisingly, lack of commitment (75%) is at the top of the list. Infidelity remains second (60%), followed by conflict (58%), getting married too young (45%), with financial problems (37%), domestic abuse (24%), and substance abuse (35%), rounding out the top seven.

The top three are quite related at their core.

To one degree or another, the couple has fallen out of love (whatever that means).
To some degree, the partners no longer expect much from the relationship.
To some degree, most of the former trust has been shredded.
The understatement of the decade. Marriages are hard.

Everyone has their own stories, but their eyes no longer light up when their partner enters the room. There is a laundry list of disappointments, unresolved issues, and unforgivenesses. Hurtful things have been said and done—on multiple occasions. There is emotional baggage and bridges burned. Trust is increasingly fragile and fluid depending on the context and topic. The proverbial grass has begun to look a lot greener. I get it—no judgment from me.

In some ways, it's a matter of brain science. As it turns out, your brain is designed by God to keep you from getting hurt again. Nothing has hurt you more than relationships gone sour. So your powerful subconscious has created offensive and defensive fortifications and strategies that have taken emotional control away from your more cautious and reasonable prefrontal cortices.

Neuroscientifically, the prefrontal cortex is the place in your brain that asks, "Hmmm, I wonder if it's a good idea to say or do that?"

If we hired a forensic team to dust for fingerprints on your recent blow-up, the harsh, hurtful words and actions, they would likely not see evidence of your prefrontal cortex anywhere near the crime scene.

Let me put it another way. Have you ever, in the heat of a 'discussion,' said something that even you were surprised came out of your mouth? It's not all your fault. In a word, you have become *reactionary*. It is a very normal part of being human—but wildly destructive to relationships.

Here's the key takeaway. Often, your brain is subconsciously working against you, bypassing the part of your frontal lobes that is at least a little bit calmer, more rational, compassionate, and even loving.

You do not have a muscle group that controls love, hate, anger, bitterness, or forgiveness. You can't just choose not to be angry, or not to be hurt, or not to be lonely, or not to want revenge. You just can't—despite what you've all been told—choose to love.

It was getting late, so I began wrapping up the conference for the evening and assigning homework to the participants.

In summary, I said, "On a relational scale of 0-10, with 10

being gracious, perfect love for your partner, and 0 being hate, we are in between on any given day. So, think of this seminar more like an AA meeting than a classroom. 'Hello, I am Richard or Amy; I do not love my spouse the way God does; I should, they deserve it.'

"You cannot just choose to stop anger, hate, bitterness, fear, and unforgivenesses.

"You cannot simply choose to love harder.

"In some ways, your brain is working against your intimacy with your partner.

"It's not *all* your fault—or theirs.

"There is hope—massive, unbelievable hope. To quote Billy Crystal as Mad Max in Princess Bride as he lifts and drops the limp arm of the dead Westley, 'I've seen worse...Turns out your friend here is only mostly dead. See, mostly dead is still slightly alive.'

"God does His best work with dead things.

I continued, "In your workbook, you will find a link to a free online love language survey. Gary Chapman's book, *The Five Love Languages: How to Express Heartfelt Commitment to Your Mate*, first published in 1992, and sold over 11 million copies in English, has been translated into 49 other languages, and the 2015 edition consistently ranks in the top 100 sellers on Amazon.com and top five books on the New York Times bestsellers list. Most of you are familiar with it and have taken the survey one or more times."

Author Side Note: Although it may not seem like it at first, I am a fan of the love languages and Dr. Chapman. I am picking on him because he is among the most familiar and successful names in Christian couples counseling. Dr. Chapman has done an excellent job of boiling down a topic fraught with emotions, dark alleys, and IEDs – relationships—making it palatable, even fun. He uses stories that most can relate to. Using simple analogies and language, he provides struggling people with a manageable to do list. Unfortunately, what the partners often do with love languages is frightening and predictable.

I completed the instructions. "Dr. Chapman helpfully observes that we have one primary love language, though we may have several. These reflect how we want or need to be loved by others. They are words of affirmation, quality time, receiving gifts, acts of service, and physical touch. I invite you to take the survey and discover your primary love language, along with #2 and #3. Write them down on the chart in your workbook. Have some fun with this.

"Then I want you to guess your partner's top three love languages. It's okay if you get it wrong—most of you will. Just do your best.

"Also, do not discuss this with your spouse. This is an individual exercise for now. Just bring your results with you in the morning. Any questions?"

❧

The next morning, I observed a very different group. It took us almost two hours, but we had each person share their love languages and hear the same from their spouses. About half of the participants seemed more upbeat, participative, and hopeful. They felt the sharing time was fun, a valuable learning experience, community-building, and memorable.

The other half of the group couldn't disagree more. They were less impressed with the topic of love languages. For them, the whole exercise exposed deep, relational rot.

When asked to share their guesses, they were rarely on point. This sometimes brought a chuckle or two, or it received a snarky look or sarcastic comment.

"So, babe, I don't know why you want more quality time. Don't I share a spot on the sofa for the Bears game every Sunday?"

Laughter

"Harry, first of all, I'm a Vikings fan!"

More laughter.

"Well, babe, we definitely need an intervention for you."

Even more laughter.

"Dear, you've checked the physical touch box, but you're just saying you want more sex."

"...And that's why I love you so much! You get me!"

"But Thel, I cleaned up after dinner last night."

"We ate out!"

"Well, yeah, but don't I get some points for taking you out?"

"I don't think Subway counts."

"My love language is service. I love it when Aaron takes the time to plan a special meal for me from start to finish. He seems to only do it when I nag him, and then it is obvious he is doing it just to shut me up."

"I guess mine is words of affirmation. I feel loved when Liz trusts me, my intelligence, expertise, and thoughts. I have run several organizations where I felt respected for who I am and the gifts I bring. But when I come home, and everything I do is questioned or undermined, or worse, when Liz talks to a friend or even a total stranger who has shaped her opinion more than me, I feel devalued and dishonored.

❧

It was time to move on. I stood, got everyone's attention, and said, "Okay, it's time for a break. We have coffee, tea, and snacks waiting for you. Please return here in 15 minutes. For the rest of the morning, we will learn how to *repent* of our love languages. Specifically, understanding how we have weaponized them."

(silence)

PRE-COUCH SIMPLE AND SURPRISING TIPS:

Remember, stop what you have been doing. I will say more.

Second, God is dancing over you and your partner. Most likely, you haven't heard that music for a long time. Just process that before the next chapter.

Third, God specializes in working with things that are mostly dead.

It's not all your or your partner's fault.

Couples, relax, you've got this. You're on a journey of discovery and growth, and you're not alone in it.

HOMEWORK:

- Watch the first season of *The Chosen* with or without your partner. Enjoy.

- Also, Google Comedian Bob Newhart's hilarious sketch, "Stop It." You will be glad you did.

QUESTIONS FOR PARTNERS TO CONSIDER

Do you think I am too hard on love languages?

What bubbled up when I said, "Stop what you were doing?" Was this helpful or just maddening?

Which reflects your current mindset?

- Impatient because I am done. I don't see anything changing that trajectory.
- Low expectations but at least I can say I gave it a try. Then my hands are clean.
- I came in with some expectation, but this approach seems a little out there. I am worried that I am wasting my time.
- I came in with little hope, but this seems different. Okay, game on.

3

TIP #2: YOUR RELATIONSHIP IS ONLY MOSTLY DEAD

"You know there is a name for people who are always wrong about everything all the time... Husband!"

— BILL MAHER

"You say you love flowers, but you cut them,
    You say you love animals, but you eat therm.
    Now you say you love me, and I'm scared."

— UNKNOWN

"Partners can be so irritating, but without them,
    who could we blame?"

— UNKNOWN

As a PASTOR for over 30 years, I have been involved in marriage counseling for many frustrated couples heading precipitously toward nasty separation and divorce. When such couples came to me, typically, it was to check the box. Someone asked them, "Did you meet with your pastor?" In Christian church-going cultures, seeking the counsel of a pastor is often a step taken before making major decisions, such as divorce.

By the time they walked into my office, the relationship was gashed, blood everywhere, breathing had virtually ceased, and, in fact, the emergency room doctor was ready to call it. They were rapidly headed toward early-onset emotional *rigor mortis*.

I am not a licensed counselor. In my early years, my approach was more typical, encompassing the standard techniques found in most marriage books, such as speaker-listener training, cognitive behavioral therapy, marriage weekends, and, of course, the five love languages.

My doctoral thesis explored what the bible really says about how to forgive others, such an important concept when it comes to marriage. I was shocked at how poorly we understood the biblical principles and instead had quickly repackaged secular notions, some of which were helpful, while others were not.

I created the Forgiving Path (www.forgivingpath.com), an online journey designed to help Christians forgive. This unique program, based on biblical principles, has helped thousands of deeply wounded Christians find a better approach to forgiveness with measurable success.

Here's what I found. Wounded partners can't just choose to forgive. We do not have that muscle group. For the same reasons, we can't choose to love, or to trust again, or reverse our belief statement, "I'm not in love with you."

The problem is that we just won't or can't do them—otherwise, we would have done them already. So, couples, relax. I won't tell you to do any of them—zero shame or guilt trips at *Before the Couch*.

My conclusion—*and this should be a comforting thought for couples*—is that your relationship, even if you categorize it as a *good* one, needs more help than you have the power to accomplish. Your marriage needs ongoing miracles and daily access to heaven-sourced capability to survive, much less thrive. Does any of that resonate?

Brilliant tools such as Dr. Chapman's love languages can—and unfortunately so often do—become destructive bats in the hands of wounded, angry, frustrated, or failing couples. It is not all Dr. Chapman's or the couples' fault. Hurting, shamed couples reach for any weapons, even good ones, to throw at their partners. Counseling couches can quickly morph into an ugly battlefield, with scattered hand-to-hand fighting and skilled sniper fire.

Let me briefly critique Dr. Chapman's love languages.

1. Most of us have a dominant 'love language' that we bring to a relationship. It may be consistent or it may change over time. It may even change depending on the context. For instance, a person who loves words of encouragement from their spouse may not feel so loved if their employer only gives them words of encouragement at raise time.

2. There is no noticeable 'love language' for Jesus.

3. There is no biblical sense that God has read Dr. Chapman's book. His love seems not to be limited or targeted according to these love languages. The Cross seems like a whole other language.

4. Empty cups can quickly latch onto love languages and become quite demanding and accusatory. Now they have the words to explain why they don't feel loved. Their spouse doesn't love them as they should.

5. Perhaps the 'Jesus-thing' to do is to lay our love languages down and die to them, so we can then experience being loved. If someone loves me and shows it in X manner, it is the sin of indifference not to receive that as real love. Why wouldn't I feel loved by it, even if it is not my specific love language?

Corollary—it is not an act of unlove to misjudge someone's love language.

❦

Let me tell you a story. The following is a composite reconstruction of dozens of couples, old and young, who sought my 'papal' blessing for their failed relationships. My approach has evolved over the decades into this simple pattern that has helped many.

Pastor: *"So welcome. I am so sorry to hear about your struggles. Marriage can be tough and brutal at times. I get it. Have a seat. We are adults here, so there's no point in beating around the bush. Carol, you told me on the phone that you want a divorce and want advice on a lawyer. Bob, this is not news to you, right?*

Carol: *I don't see any other way. We have tried to fix this. We have been to counselor after counselor. We've done marriage weekends. They all seem to say the same thing, and it just doesn't help. We are hurting each other. We are hurting the kids. I can't see any other path. I am depressed and feel like such a failure. It is best that we pull off the Band-Aid now.*

Bob: *So, at least we agree on one thing. Pastor, we are beyond the breaking point. The only reason we stayed together for so long is because of our faith and our kids. But we can't keep up this lie. I am ashamed to say that our only chance at survival is to get a divorce. We came here as a courtesy, not to have you try to change our mind—better people than you have tried. We are through.*

Bob and Carol finally sat down at the opposite ends of the couch, arms crossed, either staring at the ground or at me.

Pastor: *"Well, thanks for the courtesy of letting me know. I want to ask a few clarifying questions. This won't hurt. I will not try to talk you out of it. I don't have that kind of power. But I do have questions. I mean, two believers, followers of Christ, have come to this point? That is a big deal. Your relationship must be a huge mess. So, Bob, you first.*

18

What has happened that you would even consider a divorce from Carol? You made a vow, correct? You loved her once... that's what you said when you married her. It will affect your children for life, and after all, God hates it, right? Must be serious? What's up?"

With that invitation, Bob ranted for a time, explaining why he couldn't keep living with such a horrible person. Account after account of her criticisms, rage, selfishness, argumentativeness, inability to control spending, hurtful things said, lack of honor, how little he has felt desired by her for a long time, how he felt like he was having "sex with a corpse" (his words not mine).

After listening to him for a while, I shook my head and said,

Pastor: *"Boy, if only half of what you say is true, I couldn't stay around either."*

Then, I invited Carol to tell her side of the story. She described Bob as unforgivable, intractable, and abusive, his drinking too much, and how she has never felt desired, not really, by him. Then there is how he treated other women so much better than her. He knows that her love language is words of affirmation. "You heard him. Does that sound like affirmation?"

I sat quietly, listening, taking a few notes, and shaking my head along with her.

Pastor: *"Hmmm, Carol, I get it. If only a fraction of what you just said is true, and I do not doubt you at all, I would not want to be married to Bob, either. I get it. I wouldn't even want to hang out with him."*

"With your permission, I want to do something. It's simple—no guilt or shame. Let's call it divorce prep—or maybe pre-marriage counseling for your next relationship, or the beginning of healing for this one. Will you play along for a bit?"

They hesitantly nodded approval without glancing at each other. I asked Carol to go and rest in the waiting room for a bit. Once she left, Bob finally relaxed and uncrossed his arms.

Pastor: *"So, Bob, this is troubling. You have a huge problem. Bigger than you even think. Would you say that you dislike your spouse? How about hating her? Would you use the word despise sometimes?"*

Bob nodded slightly, clearly a bit shocked by the straightforward questions.

Pastor: *"But here's your bigger problem. This is a greater concern than you may realize. The dangerous issue is going to harm you for years to come. Your spouse is a Jesus-follower, right? Even after treating you so badly and disrespectfully for all these months and years. So, here's my question. Right now, how does God feel toward Carol?"*

Bob looked toward the ground and shook his head awkwardly.

Bob: *"Well, kind of a trick question, Pastor. Okay, I suppose that God loves her."*

Pastor: *"Even though she did what she did to you?"*

Bob: *"Of course, theologically, that's right, but..."*

Pastor: *"Not just theologically. He adores that horrible beast of a wife of yours as much as the Father loves His Son and the Son loves His Father, even though she has dishonored and treated you with disrespect. You would agree, right? God loves Carol with all the love in the universe. More than that, Jesus has already paid for all the injustices that you have felt—and more. But you aren't experiencing that right now. Here's your biggest problem. I am not discounting how big a disaster your marriage is, but it's not your priority right now. That's part of the confusion. You are out of sync with God. (pause) You hate someone that He adores. What do you make of that?"*

Bob: *"Yeah, but He is God. I am not."*

Pastor: *"Exactly right. I am glad you mentioned that. I completely agree with you. Me either. And based on what you just described, I am sure that is the tip of the iceberg. Here's the thing: I believe there's no way you could humanly love Carol. Hanging out with her and doing date nights will probably make it worse. We can do marriage counseling or a renewed contract, but your love for Carol seems dead as a doorknob to me."*

"But there is another way. It would be a miracle—a huge miracle,

the size of the parting of the Red Sea. Or better, the resurrection of Lazarus from the dead. That's a good way of seeing it. Lazarus was dead for over three days and was stinking. Your relationship stinks like a corpse. Its only hope is to be resurrected. You can't do it. It is not in you. Counseling cannot do it. Love languages—nope. You've tried. You've crashed and burned."

"But God can make *you feel love for your spouse. Did you know that? Jesus could say over your love, 'Lazarus, arise!' You would be the most surprised, wouldn't you? I am not talking about faking it till you make it, or working harder, or doing more good things. This is God making you fall in love with Carol again. Otherwise, you are both right; it is pretty dead."*

"Remember Billy Crystal as Miracle Max in The Princess Bride? 'It just so happens that your friend here is only MOSTLY dead. There's a big difference between mostly dead and all dead. Mostly dead is slightly alive. With all dead, well, with all dead, there's usually only one thing you can do...Go through his clothes and look for loose change.'"

"So let me say to you, my friend, your marriage is not actually dead, but only mostly dead."

"I am aware that you may be feeling like this is bad news. You don't want to hear it. You are ready to move on; let the mostly dead die. I understand that. So, I am asking you to do something that you will likely resist at first, but will come to accept in short order. I want you to do a simple thing for ten days. You can do this."

"Some guidelines. First, don't talk to each other unless absolutely necessary—and then just business. No 'I feel' stuff. It's too dangerous and destructive right now for mostly dead relationships. Instead, I'm going to give you a paragraph to repeat aloud twice a day for ten days. Do this individually. It will take less than a minute. That's it."

"The goal? Brother, right now, you need to feel more loved, honored, cherished, adored, appreciated, respected, and hopeful by God—as you are, not as you should be—even in this mess. It is urgent. Beyond what might or might not happen with Carol. When you begin to feel loved by

God again—I haven't mentioned Carol's love, yet—it will be a miracle of huge proportions. You desperately need such a miracle from God right now. Your being-loved cup is beat-up and leaky. That is affecting your entire life. Your future and all future relationships depend upon it."

"Don't worry about the next steps—too much for now. Just experience God's love through the Holy Spirit in your inner being. Ten days. Good? Don't do anything rash for now. Don't worry about a divorce lawyer—not just yet. It may come to that—just chill. If your spouse physically hurts you, call the police. Easy? Let's get together in ten days. Not with Carol. Just you and me. Cool?"

I handed Bob a small bookmark that we created for all Christians, but it is wildly helpful for stuck, beat-up Christians who are feeling unlovable, unloved, and unlovely.

Then, I did the same thing for Carol.

The results? Honestly, the approach does not 'save' all the marriages that shuffled lifeless into my office. But God has used it to resurrect many. The words on the bookmark have no power in and of themselves. But they do point to the source of that kind of power. Some couples continued down the path to divorce, but I believe they discovered the secret of a powerful, life-giving marriage that helped them on their next attempt. This side of heaven, we will take that.

What was on the bookmark?

PRE-COUCH EXERCISE: THE SIMPLE UNCLUTTERED GOSPEL

Like Carol and Bob, begin to say this prayer aloud to your midbrain twice a day for ten days, separate from your partner. Say it word for word. There is some scientific basis behind this simple and easy-to-do exercise. It's okay. You deserve to get a shot of Jesus' love for you. Your 'being loved, honored, and appreciated' cup is quite empty, and it leaks. You've got this.

> *"Jesus-Follower, strictly because of what Jesus did for you 2000 years ago, God actually loves you. He loves you with all His heart, as much as the Father loves the Son and the Son loves the Father. He can't love you any more or any less than He does right now—even if you were a better partner. He loves you as you are, not as you should be or could be. You can't add to this love or take away from it. Now I get it, it often feels like you've messed it up, or need to do something so God would like you better. Not so. How do you experience it more now? Simple! Good news, there is something you can do and are invited to do. You can take daily baby steps to ask the Spirit inside of you to make you know, experience, and feel just how much God loves you right now. Just ask. Ask again later today. Ask tomorrow. Make it a spiritual habit."*

Consider taking note of what jumps off the page as you say this aloud. What haven't you heard before or considered for a long time? What bothers you? What feelings bubble up? It's all good. Just keep saying it.

Couples, you've got this.

HOMEWORK:

- Google *Jireh* by Elevation Worship and Maverick City Music. Make sure it is the long play version. Grab a beverage of your choice, sit back, and let it wash over you. It's okay if you start to feel good about God's love for you. Enjoy.

QUESTIONS FOR PARTNERS TO CONSIDER

1. What did you learn that you did not know before?
2. As you listened to the composite case study, what bubbled up? Helpful or not?
3. Do you think the Simple Uncluttered Gospel can help? Why or why not?

4

TIP #3: YOU CAN'T DO IT

"Marriage is like a game of chess except the board is flowing water, the pieces are made of smoke and no move you make will have any effect on the outcome."

— COMEDIAN JERRY SEINFELD

"Getting married and becoming a father of young children has taught me that I am a narcissist. The good news is that I am a really great, really important, and really special narcissist."

— COMEDIAN JIM GAFFIGAN

WHAT DIFFERENCE DOES the Holy Spirit make in your day-to-day relationships? God created us to be relational. The Holy Spirit in your inner being is infinitely relational. Jesus taught that the inevitable and observable fruit of the Holy Spirit working is that you begin to feel love for the unlovable, the unloved, and the unlovely, including your partner and, often, including yourself.

By this all men will know that you are my disciples, if you love one another." (John 13:35)

This is important. The Holy Spirit's love looks and feels different than that of this world. It is noticeable when it pours out from you. His love is the greatest gift of the Kingdom to an increasingly polarized, racist, frightened, fractured, angry, unforgiving, lonely, and divided population. It is the thing that can rescue your relationship and take it to heights unimaginable.

We desperately need such an intervention. In the news, there seems to be daily reports of wars, war on women, on gender, on blacks, on cops, on the poor, on immigrants, on religion, on infants in the womb, and on the environment. According to Pew Research, between 1994 and 2015, the percentage of Americans in each major party who felt contempt toward those in the other party has more than tripled, from around 16% to over 50%.

Do we Christians have something different to offer?

If loving others is the most promised manifestation of the Holy Spirit in us (1 Cor 13:13), something is amiss. One of the reasons young adults are fleeing organized churches is that they don't see such a radical love happening within the four walls of congregations. Where's the Holy Spirit's patented love for each other, particularly the unlovable, unloved, and unlovely, which is all of us on any given day?

Instead, we put a great deal of energy into being *friendly* churches. That's good on paper, but it can feel fake, hypocritical, shallow, temporary, and manipulative—never miraculous. Do friendly churches need the Holy Spirit to be "friendly?"

Christians genuinely loving one another seems rare, even in friendly churches.

BIBLE STUDY

Perhaps one of the biggest reasons for the atrophy of heavenly love is that we moderns struggle to come to grips with our desperate and ongoing need of the Holy Spirit. We seem hell-bent on *working hard* on our own power. But how's that going for us?

So, the title of this chapter is *"You Can't Do It."* For now, consider stopping what you are doing. You'll see what I mean.

Check out this radical passage from Paul's letter to the Galatians.

For in Christ Jesus neither circumcision nor uncircumcision has any value. The only thing that counts is faith expressing itself through love.

— *GAL* 5:6 *NIV*

Here is some background. The Bible was clear about this for Jews. They had to be circumcised (Gen. 17:10). To not be circumcised was an affront to God Himself. Paul was picking a bit of a fight here. Here's another way to read the passage.

"For in Christ Jesus, whether you get circumcised or refuse the law and stay uncircumcised—neither choice accomplishes anything good."

In the following *Galatians 5:6 Spectrum*, there is a line with a 1-5 scale. At the far left is choosing to ignore the law, spit in God's face, and not be circumcised. The far right is to obey and be circumcised.

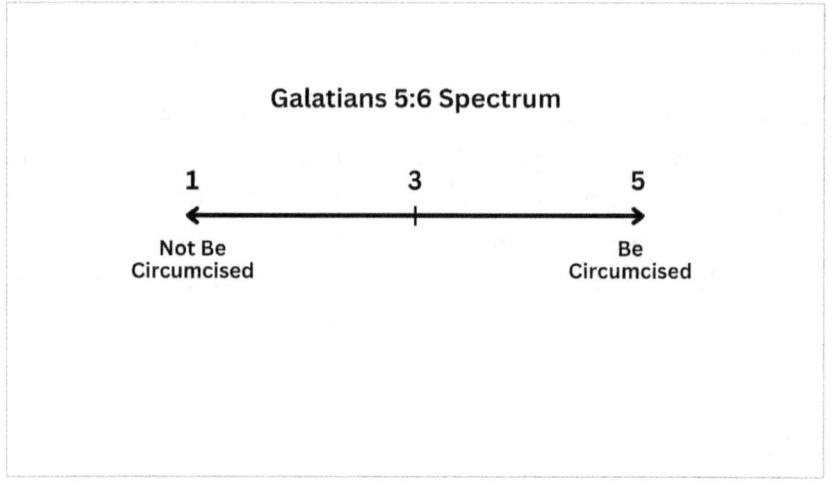

Paul is making a much larger point beyond this particular law. He is saying this about *all* laws.

Whether you keep the law—and that's a good thing to do, any law, or refuse to keep the Old Testament law, in at least one important sense the result is the same.

Remember, Paul is pro-law. He would agree that if you ignored God's commands, there are personal and societal costs—serious ones. But here he is arguing that your choices—good or bad—don't add anything to your Heavenly report card. Neither extreme adds nor takes away one iota of God's favor at all.

- Neither extreme leads anyone to God.
- Neither saves anyone.

It is the same with idolatry, lusting, stealing, or gossip. Whether you choose to obey the law and not gossip, or whether you toss the law away and gossip like crazy, neither extreme will move you closer or further away from God's arms. No doubt, internalized shame and guilt may cause you to *feel* the separation more. But neither extreme will 'save' you or cause you to lose your salvation.

So, why would you, Jesus-follower, keep the Ten Commandments? You may answer,

- "I want to please God."
- "I want to show that I am worthy of being His child."
- "I want Him to love me, the faithful child."
- "If I only did the Law, then God would love me, and my spiritual life would just skyrocket."

All typical answers, no doubt. Yet Paul is arguing that's *not* how things work. Whether you abide by the law today or ignore the law and do whatever you want, neither will make God like you more, and it will not cause your spiritual life to take off.

Let's say that this week you worked hard, a 4.5 out of 5. Is God now more pleased with you? Does He favor you more?

No.

This is amazing good news for us flawed humans. Whether you are a good Jesus-follower who works hard to obey the commands of the Bible or a poor Jesus-follower who is shoving their fist in the face of God, I can say this about you.

Solely because of Jesus' work on the Cross on your behalf, God is *already* perfectly pleased with you. Jesus did keep every single law perfectly, '5' all the time—never even a '4.99.' He only ever did the right thing—the thing that God the Father wanted him to do. His record is already mysteriously in your official dossier. God loves you as you are—technically, in a very narrow human sense, He *must*. It is a fact that God loves sinners. That's all there is.

But isn't keeping the law the right thing to do? Yes and no. Trick question. It is more complicated than it appears at first blush. *Doing* the right things is not the fulfillment of the law. The Pharisees did many things right. They worked hard at it.

The essential aspect of the law is that you should *want* to love

God and love your neighbor, including your faulty partner. It is entirely possible to *do* the right things and still feel nothing for others. You may still see them as a nuisance.

The law requires that you *want* to love your partner, not because you must. Those are two very different things. *Wanting* to love is more difficult than *choosing* to love.

More good news. God knows your innate inability to love others, particularly those irritating people in your life. Paul goes on:

> *The only thing that counts is faith expressing itself through love.*

> — GAL 5:6

Or equally translated is,

> On the other hand, the only thing that works is "faith," which innately makes love happen. (i.e., manufactures love)

He is not talking about you trying harder to 'faith'—whatever that conjures up in your brain.

The faith he is referring to is *of* the Holy Spirit in you. His heavenly-sourced 'faith' generates a love way beyond your capability—way more powerful than your scrawny old, shriveled, hard-raisin heart can produce. He does so from within your inner being, wherever that is.

The Holy Spirit's faith is designed to unleash such love in you and through you. It floods your uneasy, dysfunctional, beat-up, suspicious, careful, guarded, boundary-riddled heart with something dramatically new and powerful—His love for you and, as importantly, His love for your hard-to-love, irritating other.

Let's adjust the *Galatians 5:6 Spectrum* to speak to our relationships. Using the same spectrum, but instead of circumcision, we have *I'm done with my partner* at '1' on the scale and *I'm working hard to love my partner because I have to* at '5.'

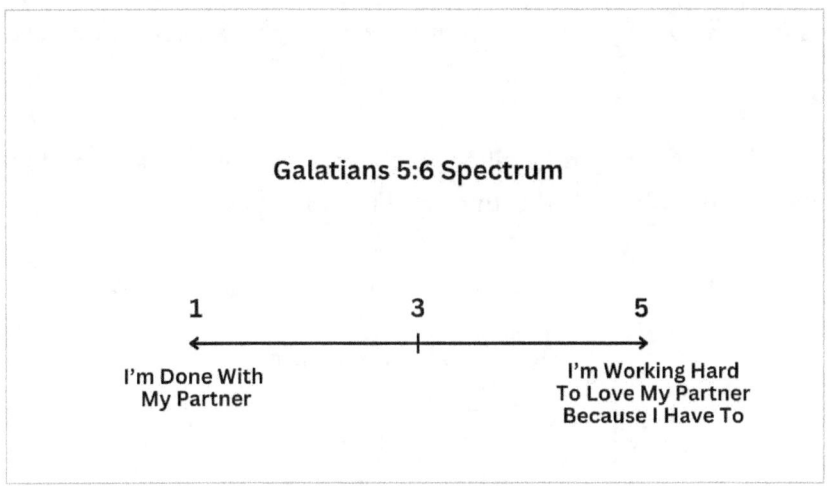

Galatians 5:6 Spectrum

If you are at or near '1,' you may feel like you're ready to call it quits with your partner. You have your reasons. They may have mistreated you abusively, and you figure they deserve it. In one sense, you hate them. You likely blame them for the mess and your raw feelings. You can hardly imagine living with them for one more day. Even though Jesus loves them with all the love in the universe and commands you to love them, you've tried. You can't. You won't.

On the other side of the spectrum is '5.' You will do the *right thing* and continue to work as hard as you can, counseling, learning about love languages, attending conference after conference, reading book after book. But you are miserable and increasingly resentful to be stuck in this untenable situation.

For most, you are not at '1' or '5' but somewhere in between. Your efforts are likely hit or miss. You are trying, but with limited expectations.

You probably expect this book to lay a heavy guilt trip on you. "If you are at '3,' I want you to try harder, to lean into choosing to love your spouse. Ask God to help you get to '4.'

I am not going to do that. Remember Gal 5:6? Christians, you have an amazing Plan B.

The Holy Spirit can perform a miracle in you that makes you want to love the unlovable.

That is the nature of all of God's love. He only loves the unlovable, the unlovely, and the unloved. That's all of us.

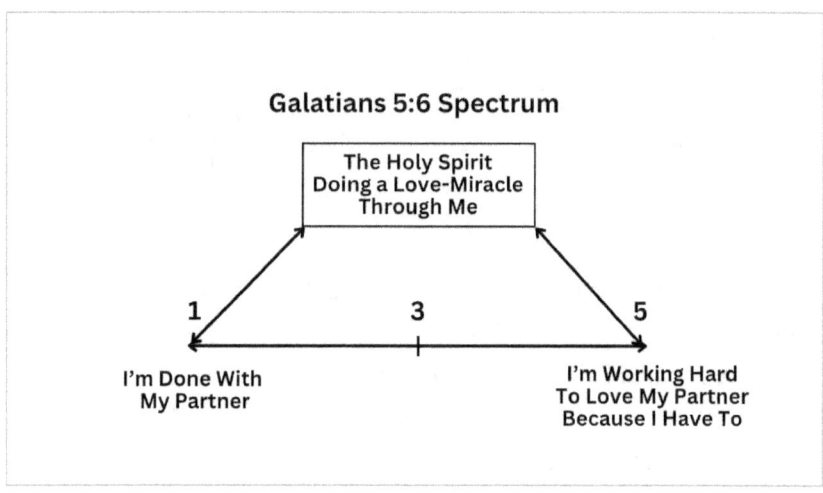

Check out this new diagram. Whether you hate the person (1) or try hard to do what you know God wants you to do (5)—neither works—not well anyway. Neither option on the typical human spectrum accomplishes anything miraculous, nor does it have Kingdom fingerprints.

But you have a very powerful Plan B. See the box placed off and above the usual spectrum labelled "The Holy Spirit Doing a Love Miracle Through Me."

Look up and **ask** the Holy Spirit in you to do such a miracle to *make* you love the other with *His* love.

Listen to Gal 5:6 expanded.

For those of you who are in Christ (those in whom the Spirit of Christ dwells, the same Spirit who has at his fingertips the height, width, length, and depth of the love of Christ toward you and the person that you don't care for right now), whether you choose to do the right thing and stretch your Saran wrap thin love over the porcupiny other —or whether you choose the opposite, hate them, accuse them, justify your anger and rage, avoid them, slander them to others, or silently hope they get crushed—in a real sense doesn't matter. Neither extreme has the capacity to accomplish loving the other—meaning, making you actually love them or them feeling loved. This does not further the Kingdom in any way. Don't think that because you do something that looks like loving (choose to forgive, choose to be compassionate, choose to pursue, choose to use their love language, etc.), you are actually loving the other person or have the power to forgive them or reconcile with them, or that your love will change them in any way. It won't. It does not have the power. Fortunately, there is another way for Spirit-filled Jesus followers. The Holy Spirit within you can overwhelm you with His powerful, superhuman faith, which is innately all about one thing—making you feel the love for yourself that Jesus paid for and feel a deep love for your irritating, unlovable partner. That is what the Holy Spirit's faith does. It makes love happen within you and has more than a decent shot at making it felt—at least noticed—by the other.

So, if you don't love someone that God loves, you have a legitimate choice. You can admit that such a love is just not in your toolbox—never was. Then, ask the Holy Spirit to fill you with His faith, which will begin to make you feel love for the other. It's your choice. This is the heavenly love Jesus spoke about that causes people to see and say, "Hey, they are a follower of Jesus—how else would they do that?" But please, stop thinking and bragging that you can love your partner with the love God commands on your own. Nothing could be further from the truth.

SUMMARY:

God can give you access to power that will extend beyond the horizontal DIY love spectrum. He has the capacity to give you His motivation, desire, and power to love the unlovable. That is what He innately does. He can give you "faith," which by nature *makes* such a ridiculous love happen.

God can make you feel love for your partner who has hurt you, let you down, and who doesn't make your heart zing like it used to. Jesus could say over your mostly dead love, "Lazarus, arise! Love arise!" Wouldn't you be the most surprised?

In heaven, I guarantee you will love each other even more than you ever have. What's the difference? Is it the place—Heaven? No. It is that you will finally be fully immersed in the power of the Holy Spirit and will at last fully experience the height, width, depth, and length of the love of Jesus toward you *and* your spouse.

This *may* sound like bad news. You may have already decided to move on; let the mostly dead be dead. I get it—pretty human, I think. If so, something inside you may revile against spending one more second on your current toxic relationship.

Nevertheless, I am asking you to do something relatively simple for ten days. First, don't talk to your partner unless you must—and even then, just business. You are welcome. No "I feel" stuff. It's too dangerous and destructive right now for mostly dead, toxic relationships.

Instead, say the *Make Me Prayer* below over and over—to yourself—*for* yourself. Say it twice a day for at least ten days. Right now, *you* need to feel loved, honored, cherished, adored, appreciated, respected, and hopeful by God again, as you are, even in your current mess. It is an urgent need.

"God, right now I am hurting, depressed, angry, feeling disrespected, unloved, hopeless, beat-up, feeling ashamed and like a failure...and that's just the tip of the iceberg. I really don't like this person. I wish I had never known them. To some degree, I despise them. I am also afraid of them. I can't take it being with them, being near them anymore. My body has a visceral reaction when I am in the same room. Honestly, I am at the end of my rope. I admit that You love them as they are, even after all the things they did to me and the many things they didn't do for me. I don't. I confess I am way out of sync with You. This frightens me. Honestly, I am afraid You can make me love them again. I am not sure at all that I want that to happen. I am done. However, I am willing to come to You to ask that You make me feel loved by You again. I need that. I want that desperately. Holy Spirit, unleash Your faith in my inner being and make love happen for me. Now, please. Amen."

As you begin to feel loved by God again, dance a little. Don't worry about the next steps. It is too much for now. Just be immersed in the love of God through the Holy Spirit in your inner being. Sound good? Also, don't do anything rash for now. Chill. As always, if your partner physically hurts you, call the police. You have my permission.

Then, if you are ready, try adding the following little prayer. If not, no judgment. Just keep on saying the first prayer as long as it takes. When you are ready, pray this.

Holy Spirit, I am also begging that You give me Your love for them. This is hard right now. I am not sure I really want it. This is scary. So, give me Your perfect love that casts out fears. Give me wisdom so I don't do something foolish. Amen.

Say the prayers at least twice a day. When you feel your blood pressure rise, say the prayers. When you think of the person and feel fear, depression, or rage, say the prayers.

Do you still need professional counseling? Cognitive Behavioral Therapy? Emotionally Focused Therapy? Marriage contracts? Love languages? Conflict skills? Yes, of course, no doubt.

But at this point, before the couch, what you need most is the Holy Spirit's power to *make* love happen within you. You cannot do that. You cannot choose to 'love' any more than you can choose to fly. So, stop trying.

What if your partner is not a Christian? That is a good and relevant question. Hear Jesus Himself.

In the same way, let your light shine before others, that they may see your good deeds and glorify your Father in heaven.

— MATT 5:16

What is Jesus saying? Imagine some unbelieving stranger who happens to observe how you treat your unlovable partner with ridiculous heaven-sourced love and kindness. Jesus says that the Spirit's love through you is so powerful and so clearly alien that they may be shocked and moved by it, causing them to hit their knees right there and praise God, the God they didn't even believe in a moment before. They become converted, seeing God's love through you.

In their brain, they are thinking, "Oh my word, there must be a God for that kind of love to exist. I haven't seen anything like this in any faith expression anywhere. I praise that God. I'm in."

When we participate in the Holy Spirit's work, we are involved with very powerful, life-changing activities. When you ask Him, the hope is that He will work such shocking, unimaginable miracles in you and through you. Not parlor tricks, big miracles, like loving your partner.

It's comparable to 'Lazarus, come forth!'

PRE-COUCH EXERCISE #1:

Begin to say this chapter's prayers, one or both, aloud twice a day for ten days, separate from your partner. Say it word for word. There is some scientific basis behind this simple and easy-to-do exercise. As we said in the last chapter, you deserve to get a shot of Jesus' love for you. All we did with these prayers was to ramp up the rhetoric a bit. Likely, it resonates with some part of your midbrain. You are not alone, and it is not all your fault. You've got this.

PRE-COUCH EXERCISE #2:

Check out Comedian Sinbad's hilarious 'Marriage is Work' on YouTube.

QUESTIONS FOR PARTNERS TO CONSIDER

1. What did you hear that was new to you? Helpful?
2. The author made a clear distinction between asking God to *help* you versus asking God to *make* you. What is the difference? Is it troubling that God can make you do something like that?

3. Related question. What would God have to *make* happen in you before a change in your relationship might become noticeable? At this point, you don't have to believe that he will. No judgment.

5

TIP #4: FEELING LONELY IS NOT ALL YOUR PARTNER'S FAULT

—OR YOURS

"We were made, not primarily that we may love God (though we were made for that too), but that God may love us."

— C.S. LEWIS

"Grace, it turns out, is not an idea or a thing but a radical, divine dynamic."

— JOHN BARCLAY

"I FEEL *SO* LONELY SOMETIMES," Laura said with great sincerity; her glance at her husband, Zach, revealed who she felt was to blame.

Laura's experience is not unique. According to the 2023 Surgeon General's report, only a paltry 39% of adults in the U.S. reported feeling deeply connected to others. Approximately half of U.S. adults reported experiencing loneliness, with the highest rates observed among young adults. Millennials (age 28-43) score 43.3% on the UCLA Loneliness Scale. Gen Zs (age 16-27) score a staggering 48.3%.

This level of loneliness is more detrimental to your health than obesity and is equivalent to smoking fifteen cigarettes a day. This epidemic of loneliness will reverberate for decades and has immeasurable adverse effects on all our relationships.

Rachael Wurzman captures the threat of loneliness related to addictions.

"Think of it like this. Loneliness creates a hunger in the brain, and our brains signal deep dissatisfaction. We become restless, irritable, and impulsive. If we don't have the ability to connect socially, we are so ravenous for our social neurochemistry to be rebalanced, we're likely to seek relief from anywhere. And if that anywhere is opioid painkillers or heroin, it is going to be a heat-seeking missile for our social rewards system. Is it any wonder people in today's world are becoming addicted so easily?"[1]

Let's return to Laura and Zach. No one is questioning Laura's honesty. I am sure she does feel lonely, and I suspect Zach does as well. Loneliness is a massive problem today and has been since Eve and Adam took a bite out of the forbidden fruit. The issue is not whether loneliness exists or whether Laura feels it. The question is, where does it originate?

Think of a loneliness spectrum ranging from 1 to 5. On one side is "I feel lonely because Zach is ignoring me—or not pursuing me—or spends more time in the office than he used to—or is into porn, or regularly flirts with other women, or fill in the blank." On the opposite side is, "I feel lonely because my own companionship and intimacy cup is empty, and I see that it leaks."

1. Wurzman, Rachael. (December 13, 2019). TED Radio Hour: Can Social Isolation Lead to Opioid Addiction.

So, when Laura says, 'I feel lonely,' where is her experience on the spectrum? Is she blaming Zach's behavior or motivation toward her as the problem? Or is she confessing something lacking in her core being, or somewhere in between?

Loneliness can be understood as a fruit and a root—most likely some combination of both on a very fluid loneliness spectrum. I am not suggesting that Zach is off the hook, not at all. I am suggesting that Zach is not the whole problem. Neither is Laura.

As true with most spectrums, the reality is almost always somewhere between 1 and 5. Unfortunately, my experience has shown me that it is far easier to blame our partner and move on.

The bigger problem is usually internal and related to past relational fragmentation that has been hardwired in our brains by every good and bad relationship we have experienced.

To one degree or another, past issues and relationships have contributed to your present, valid feelings of loneliness and are not all your fault or your spouse's.

What are the chances that Laura—and Zach, for that matter—came to the relationship needing the other to help them feel less lonely?

"One of the reasons I was attracted to Zach, at least in those early months," confessed Laura, "was that he made me feel special, attractive, lovable, and, of course, less lonely."

Many of us have an unfortunate notion that our spouse or partner is supposed to be the cure for our loneliness. That is only partly true.

The bigger problem is that post-fall, almost every relationship on the planet involves two loneliness-prone people who both expect the other to make them feel less lonely. You've likely heard the metaphor that bad marriages are like two ticks sucking blood from each other. Honestly, most would fit that picture.

Good news. Christians can access a better source of an anti-loneliness potion, and we need to access it regularly for the sake of our relationships.

Neurologically, loneliness is very real. It is an actual pain experienced in the exact location of your brain, as with any other physical pain. To some degree, one could treat loneliness medicinally with pain relievers. Some suggest the opioid crisis is partly driven by the epidemic rise in loneliness and isolation.

When you feel lonely, take two Advil. It might help, but you risk becoming addicted to Advil.

Other than taking Advil and blaming our partners, what can we do?

CONSIDER GRACE

We all know about grace. We are saved by it. Over half a millennium after the Great Reformation, most Christians have become familiar with the phrase, 'sola gratia,' by grace alone. But what is grace?

Grace is the free and *unmerited* favor of God manifested in the salvation of sinners and the bestowal of blessings.

Amen. But do we know what that is saying? Who talks that way? Very few use the term 'favor' anymore.

In my research on grace, I observed that the emphasis is on the word "unmerited." We did nothing to earn it; we don't deserve it. Grace is ours strictly because of Jesus and his efforts on our behalf. Amen.

The bulk of theologians discuss how grace is accessed, specifically the "means of grace" (i.e., sacraments, faith, prayer, fasting).

Great, but what *is* 'grace?' What difference does it make for lonely Laura or Zach?

To put it in popular terms, what is so amazing about grace?

Many Christians tend to think of grace as a heavenly commodity. You are feeling lonely or going through a troubled stretch in your life, so you turn to God and ask for 'grace' like you would order a helpful elixir from Amazon. The idea is that when it arrives, you open the box, drink the bottle, and immediately feel better.

Others treat grace more like a battery or a power source. Grace plugs me into Jesus' power to thrive, overcome sin, and feel better about my life.

Neither of those images is totally wrong per se—but alone, they fall way short of the biblical nature of real grace.

The Bible has a much higher view of grace, and one that is of far greater value to Laura and Zach.

Paul writes,

"All this is for your benefit, so that the grace that is reaching more and more people may cause thanksgiving to overflow to the glory of God."

— 2 COR 4:15

Paul imagines grace as a living sentient entity that is actively reaching more and more needy people. But it does more than embrace. The people are dramatically changed. The touch of grace miraculously causes gratefulness and the desire to worship God to bubble up within them. Not just a little. The Greek implies that grace caused something to exist that wasn't there before, and a lot of it. So, one moment, it wasn't there, and the next, there was too much —spilling out all over the place. That's the DNA of grace. Not exactly what 'favor' communicates. Grace is a powerful force which is noticeable and transformative.

❦

How might that change Laura and Zach's relationship?

The author of Hebrews warns Christians not to squander the availability of grace.

"See to it that no one misses the grace of God and that no bitter root grows up to cause trouble and defile many."

— *HEB 12:15*

In the Greek, it says, "Be very careful so you don't miss out on the value of grace through your own lack of effort."

If you fail to take advantage of this amazing grace regularly, you will start to feel bitter toward God and others. You may see other joyful Christians and wonder what's wrong with you.

Here's Paul again.

"And God is able to make all grace abound to you, so that in all things at all times, having all that you need, you will abound in every good work."

— *2 COR 9:8*

Paul might write, "Laura, God is powerful enough to make you feel every bit of His grace, not only in drips and drabs but so much that you will feel overwhelmed by it. Anytime, anyplace, especially when you feel lonely, you will have all the grace you ever need. One more thing. There will be so much of the stuff that you won't be able to contain it. It will *have* to overflow from your gut in the form of good works toward others. You will necessarily even become a source of grace for Zach."

In Acts 6:5, Luke describes Stephen as being full of faith and the Holy Spirit. In vs. 8, Luke describes him as being full of God's grace and power.

"This proposal pleased the whole group. They chose Stephen, a man full of <u>faith</u> and of the <u>Holy Spirit</u> ... Now Stephen, a man <u>full of God's grace</u> and <u>power</u>, did great wonders and miraculous signs among the people."

— ACTS 6:5-8

Luke would have us understand grace as being intimately aligned with the person of the Holy Spirit Himself. I suggest that grace, among other things, is a synonym for the intimate presence of the Holy Spirit and His innate workings in us. In virtually every passage where this powerful grace is mentioned, you could replace it with the Holy Spirit. Grace is manifested wherever the Spirit is. Wherever the Spirit is, there is grace. It is his relational DNA experienced by beat-up, lonely, and needy people.

The word for 'grace,' *charis*, at its core, is a relational term. Some scholars believe it comes from the European root meaning "to like, pursuing love or desire." If the Holy Spirit '*charises*' you, you *will* feel loved and pursued. You would notice.

He is the one personally reaching hurting, self-focused people and making them grateful. He fills lonely and bitter people with His motivation and gifts. He is making people like Laura and Zach feel loved and lovable—and, of course, less lonely.

When I teach this in churches, I often invite a person to join me up front. I tell the person that after two scenes, I want them to tell me which one they prefer.

In the first role play, I take on the persona of an Amazon delivery person. I knock on the person's door.

"Special delivery from God. You ordered some Amazing Grace. Yeah? OK, it's all paid for, shipping and handling. Just sign here."

In the second role play, I take on the persona of the Holy Spirit. With their permission, I hug them profusely.

"I saw that you were down and beat up, lonely, feeling like an underachiever. You are in a tough place. But I came to tell you just how special you are to me. I wouldn't pick anyone else—just you. You are the entire package. I am so proud of you. I can't believe the young woman or man you've grown into. I can't wait to spend more time with you. It will be great. Just a little more you need to do. You'll see why. Remember, I am with you always—I can't stop looking into your eyes. I definitely picked just the right color."

In which scenario do you think the person feels more *charised* or loved?

WHY DO WE NEED THIS?

Theologian John Calvin explains why we need to diligently ask the Holy Spirit to lavish us with grace daily.

"So why do believers feel such anxiety and fears related to their relationship with God? Why do we have so many violent temptations that keep coming to our brains, unending wave after wave, that inevitably cause us to doubt God's goodness, God's love for us, and our position as His child? Why doesn't faith give us more ongoing certainty? Why don't we feel stunning confidence and assurance of God's adoration all the time? For reasons known only to God, on this side of heaven, we are not promised certainty and assurance of our relational attachment to God that is never affected by fears, doubt, shame, or anxiety. We are saved into a lifetime of struggle with our

dysfunctional consciences, which spew out fears and doubts. This is our charge: to learn to be aware of our struggle and to lean into faith to overcome our inner doubts and fears more regularly. This side of heaven, our consciences will never be still or fear and anxiety-free."[2]

— JOHN CALVIN (EXPANDED)

Let me ask: if Laura was lavished with grace, how might it affect her feelings about herself, her worth, and her *enoughness*?

One author writes about our need for enoughness.

"Listen carefully and you'll hear [the] word 'enough' everywhere, especially when it comes to the anxiety, loneliness, exhaustion, and division that plague our moment to such tragic proportions. You'll hear about people scrambling to be successful enough, happy enough, thin enough, wealthy enough, influential enough, desired enough, charitable enough, woke enough, good enough. We believe instinctively that, were we to reach some benchmark in our minds, then value, vindication, and love would be ours."[3]

— *DAVID ZAHL- SECULOSITY*

How might grace affect Laura's relationship with Zach?

Robert Robinson was born to Michael and Mary Robinson in 1735. His parents' romance was one for the ages. True love. Something that John Donne or Elizabeth Barrett Browning might write about. But

---

2. Calvin, John. *Institutes of the Christian Religion*. Translated by Henry Beveridge, Hendrickson Publishers, 2008, Book 3, Chapter 2, Section 17. paraphrased.
3. Zahl, David. *Seculosity: How Career, Parenting, Technology, Food, Politics, and Romance Became Our New Religion and What to Do about It*. Fortress Press, 2019.

sadly, it turned out to be a Shakespearian tragedy—a replay of Romeo and Juliet. A love that could never be.

Robert's mom was of the wealthy London upper crust. His dad, not so much. Well, you know what happened. Robert's mother was disowned. Cast out of her family. They fell into deep poverty. It got worse. His dad passed away when he was five. Robert and his mom struggled to survive.

It got even worse. Robert's grandfather took one last shot at his daughter, even on his deathbed—one last wounding. In the will, young Robert was awarded ten shillings and a sixpence, virtual pocket change—someone estimated $6.50 in today's money.

Robert had every right to be bitter, cynical, unforgiving, and angry.

But in the 1750s, the Holy Spirit intervened and flooded the beat-up lad with a tsunami wave of grace. It was the Great Awakening, and the Holy Spirit's power was sweeping through Europe and the colonies. Robert happened to hear the great preacher George Whitefield. Robert got 'graced.'

What changed? When this bitter and angry young man finally looked up into Jesus' eyes, Robert was no longer a shamed, publicly disinherited, and dishonored orphan anymore. His identity was no longer based on how his maternal grandfather had treated him. His value was no longer dependent on heroically picking up the fragmented pieces of his life. His value came from an experience of the Holy Spirit's love for the unlovable, the unloved, and the unlovely.

Robert's real patriarch in heaven loved him as he was with all the love in the universe, not as he should have been or could have been. His real, irrevocable inheritance of grace was far greater than ten shillings and sixpence.

You may not recognize his name, but Robert is the author of the great hymn "Come Thou Fount of Many Blessings."[4] Notice the

---

4. Robinson, R. (1758). Come, Thou Fount of Every Blessing.

wording and the stark difference between the inheritance he might humanly claim he deserved, and the stunning, unimaginable inheritance he was given that he did not deserve.

> *Come Thou Fount of every blessing*
> *Tune my heart to sing Thy grace;*
> *Streams of mercy, never ceasing,*
> *Call for songs of loudest praise*
> *Teach me some melodious sonnet,*
> *Sung by flaming tongues above.*
> *Praise the mount! I'm fixed upon it,*
> *Mount of God's unchanging love.*
> *Jesus sought me when a stranger,*
> *Wandering from the fold of God;*
> *He, to rescue me from danger,*
> *Interposed His precious blood;*

So different from how his grandpa and the world treated him.

> *How His kindness yet pursues me*
> *Mortal tongue can never tell,*
> *Clothed in flesh, till death shall loose me*
> *I cannot proclaim it well.*
> *O to grace how great a debtor*
> *Daily I'm constrained to be!*

Grace: The power to really know, to really feel how much God loves you as you are right now—no matter what side of the tracks you are on.

> *Let that grace now like a fetter,*
> *Bind my wandering heart to Thee.*

But I keep forgetting. I desperately need to preach the gospel of grace to myself over and over.

> *Prone to wander, Lord, I feel it,*
> *Prone to leave the God I love;*
> *Here's my heart, O take and seal it,*
> *Seal it for Thy courts above.*

PRE-COUCH EXERCISE:

Ask the Holy Spirit to immerse your midbrain with His powerful and overflowing grace. Continue until you feel like dancing.

HOMEWORK:

- Go to The Beltones *Come Thou Fount* on YouTube. Please sit back, grab a beverage of choice, and drink it in. Full disclosure: I am a proud father—my daughter is third from the right in the front row.

PRAY:

Holy Spirit, quick, give me Your amazing grace so I can begin to noticeably feel Your unbelievable love for me and others right now, quick, before I do something stupid. Amen.

Pray this a couple of times today, a couple of times tomorrow, and the next day. You just might notice a difference. Others will, too.

Couples, you've got this. Are you beginning to experience something new?

QUESTIONS FOR PARTNERS TO CONSIDER

1. What did you hear that was new to you? Helpful?
2. Is the author saying that your partner is off the hook? Explain. What good is it if the Holy Spirit can make you feel less lonely but your partner is still a selfish jerk?
3. When will we get the list of things we need to do? Thoughts?
4. Most Important Question. Doesn't my daughter have a great voice?

6

TIP #5: THE REASON YOU FEEL STUCK AND POWERLESS IS YOU ARE

—AND IT'S NOT ALL YOUR FAULT.

"When I get honest, I admit I am a bundle of paradoxes. I believe and I doubt, I hope and get discouraged, I love and I hate, I feel bad about feeling good, I feel guilty about not feeling guilty. I am trusting and suspicious. I am honest and I still play games. Aristotle said I am a rational animal; I say I am an angel with an incredible capacity for beer."

— BRENNAN MANNING

SAMANTHA, like many of us, feels trapped in her relationship with Jamal—stuck, helpless, and powerless. She's tried to bridge the gap with love languages. Jamal's language is acts of service—hers is quality time, and a close second is words of encouragement. These were not modeled in Jamal's family of origin, and he seems lost. Bottom line, despite her efforts to please Jamal, she only feels increasingly empty. She's indeed bitter and frustrated and wonders if it's all a big mistake.

POWERLESSNESS

Here are some very encouraging words for Samantha—and Jamal—from the Apostle Paul in Eph 3:14.

> *"For this reason, I kneel before the Father, from whom his whole family in heaven and on earth derives its name. I pray that out of his glorious riches he may strengthen you with power through his Spirit in your inner being..."*

This is ridiculously good news. 'Name' can stand for significance, identity, worth, purpose, value, the thing that makes you really you, which others notice and appreciate. From where does Paul remind the Ephesians (and Samantha and Jamal) that their core significance derives? Is it their choices? Careers? Relationship? DNA? Their families of origin? Their good works? Their religion? Love languages? What they think the other feels about them today? What they feel about themselves today?

No. Biblically, our core sense of worth, value, and lovability is from God. This is a deeply comforting truth. If we truly internalize this, we would need less 'name' from our partners—meaning less strain on the relationship, less frustration, less feeling unloved, and fewer reactionary arguments that cause more harm than good.

Does this make sense?

Paul goes on to say, *"I pray that out of His glorious riches he may strengthen you with power through His Spirit in your inner-being..."*

Paul wants each of the Ephesians—every one of them—the good and the not-so-good, the young and old, couples and singles—every one of them—to feel the very power of God in their inner being today and tomorrow.

Three times in this section, Paul acknowledges their feelings of powerlessness and need for an alien power.[1] Why would they feel powerless? It may be the same reason that Samantha does. No matter what she tries, it bears paltry fruit.

For Paul, the key for individuals and couples is to stop trying harder through their own efforts and begin to access God's heavenly power immediately.

Samantha, when was the last time you felt such a power from God in your inner being—and knew it? Or in your relationship? It seems that Paul is speaking of an ongoing feeling of such power—as if their very present and future depended upon it.

It does.

THREE 'SO THATS'

The power that comes from God accomplishes three things in our lives. First, we need the power of God *so that* "Christ may dwell in your hearts through faith." (17)

Have you ever wondered if you were still a Christian? Perhaps you strayed from God and the church. You wonder if God still cares. Or maybe He is disappointed? You are beginning to hear those 'I am afraid' statements bubbling up.

> "I am afraid I am not good enough for God."
> "I am afraid God won't say to me, 'Well done, good and faithful servant, enter into your rest."
> "I am afraid Jesus is disappointed in me."

None of those statements are true. And yet, would it surprise you to know that you are not alone? I asked two congregations to share their fears related to God. Over two-thirds voiced the very same fears.

---

1. Paul uses two different Greek very similar words for power, dunamis (vs. 16, 20) and exischuo (v. 18).

Paul reminds us that we can access a power from God specifically designed to make the Samanthas of the world feel like a child of God in good favor today. Wouldn't it be amazing and life-changing for you to hear God the Father say, "You are my beloved child with whom I am well pleased? I adore you as much as I love my Son, and He loves me."

Second, God's power is the only thing capable of reprogramming your dulled midbrain *so that* it will "begin to grasp how wide and long and high and deep is the love of Christ and to know this love that surpasses knowledge" (18).

This is clearly not a theoretical or philosophical 'grasp.' Of course, you know in your prefrontal cortex that Jesus loves you. Paul is talking about really experiencing it. That is what Samantha wants from Jamal. Here, she can get it from God Himself—the same love that innately loves the unlovable, the unloved, and the unlovely.

Samantha, surely that would make a massive difference in your sense of being loved and appreciated.

Third *so that*, God's power makes emptied and leaky cups—like Samantha's—"filled to the measure of all the fullness of God."(18)

What does it mean to be filled with the fullness of God? I'm not sure. However, it certainly includes a different kind of satisfaction as God's presence fills the many nasty gaps, cracks, wounds, hunger, hurts, anxieties, fears, and insecurities Samantha brought to the relationship with Jamal in the first place. That's glorious fullness, for sure. It would be noticeable.

Paul's key concern was that the Ephesians were doing good things on behalf of Jesus without first being filled with the necessary power from God. The technical term for what they were doing was 'religion.'

Christians attempt to do many 'Godly things' by their own power, but in the end, they burn out because they fear they haven't done nearly enough to earn God's love. It is, of course, horrible theology, yet we all do it.

Paul was right. In the end, at Jesus' tragic performance review of the Ephesian church, he summed up their failure in a single phrase, "You have forsaken your first love." Rev 2:4

Samantha is on the very same trajectory. As are so many Christians.

THE GOSPEL APP SHAPE

Let me illustrate how necessary the Holy Spirit's power is to Samantha and Jamal with this helpful Gospel App Shape.

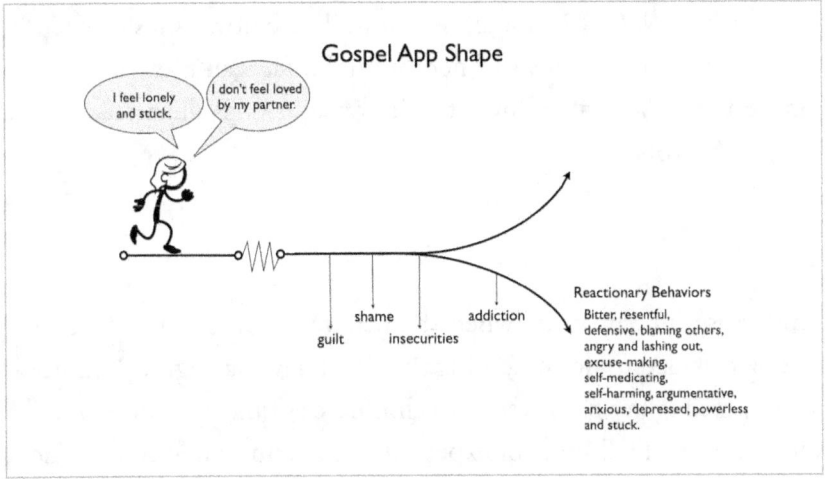

For now, let's have the stick figure on the left represent Samantha —but it could equally be Jamal. Samantha is struggling in her relationship with Jamal, and unless there is some powerful intervention, she is most likely going to take the downward lower curve toward her hardwired reactionary behaviors. Why? She is dissatisfied, frustrated, and stuck—still tirelessly striving to do the right thing in her relationship. How is that working for her?

Does Jamal love her? She's not sure. God loves her, but she generally goes through life blissfully unaware, often feeling unlovable, and some days working hard with little fruit. Other days, she throws up her hands and gives up.

To the far lower right are some of Samantha's typical reactionary feelings and behaviors. It is not all her fault. At the end of a hard day, trying to be loved by her own wiles, she can be bitter, resentful, defensive, and filled with rage. She might blame Jamal, lash out, make excuses, self-medicate, self-harm (over/undereating, cutting, etc.), fight back, and experience anxiety, depression, or powerlessness.

It gets worse. Samantha's midbrain has several downward subconscious powers that make it even more difficult for her to love others, to feel empathy and compassion, and yes, even to feel their love for her. Note it is not all her fault. These powers reside deep in the subconscious shadows of her midbrain. She can't just 'choose' to ignore them. We will address the four major ones illustrated in the Gospel App Shape.

GUILT

Guilt arises in Samantha when she believes she has done something wrong or failed to do something that she knew was right. Remorse is a nasty feeling her brain wants to eliminate as quickly as possible. She messed up and fell short of expectations, missing some commitment or promise. It has blunted her ability to feel loved and to love.

Some core belief statements accelerate Samantha's decline into under-the-curve, guilt-reactionary behaviors.

"I cannot do enough right things to make Jamal appreciate me. That must be why he has pulled away. He is right. I messed up again. It's my fault."

Samantha will tend to spin into reactionary behaviors, which do not achieve her goal of attaining the love she wants or needs.

SHAME

The second downward power in Samantha's brain that affects her sense of self-worth and relationships is shame. Shame is far worse than guilt. It's not only that she messed up; shame whispers to her midbrain that she *is* a mess-up. Listen to how Brené Brown talks about shame.

> "Think back to when we were children or young adults, and we first learned how important it is to be liked, to fit in, and to please others. The lessons were often taught by shame; sometimes overtly, other times covertly. Regardless of how they happened, we can all recall experiences of feeling rejected, diminished and ridiculed. Eventually, we learned to fear these feelings. We learned how to change our behaviors, thinking and feelings to avoid feeling shame. In the process, we changed who we were and, in many instances, who we are now."

Our internalized shame is a dangerous power that can make Samantha feel unworthy of genuine love, of life-giving relationships, or of being noticed and honored for who she truly is. Shame can cause her to believe her core connection to Jamal and God has unraveled, leading to depression, anxiety disorders, addiction, eating disorders, bullying, suicide, and all types of violence, including family violence.

Let's unpack some of Samantha's negative shame belief statements.

"I am inadequate."
"I am worthless. I have no intrinsic value; that must be why Jamal has treated me so cruelly. What other reason could there be?"
"I am broken...There seems to be something wrong with me,

a deep-seated *ugly* that sets me apart and subjects me to disdain, shaking heads, eyes that turn away, judgmental chuckles from others."

"I am unlovable...Look at me; why would Jamal feel drawn to me, like what he sees, want to be with me, or to let me into his heart?"

INSECURITIES

The third internalized power that drags Samantha down is residual insecurities. I have written extensively on the Attachment Theory. Please visit my FREE online course, Good Enough Parent (www. goodenoughparent.online), for a more in-depth look.

Whether you know it or not, both you and your partner have deeply hardwired inner-working models in your midbrain that largely drive your behaviors, especially your reactionary behaviors.

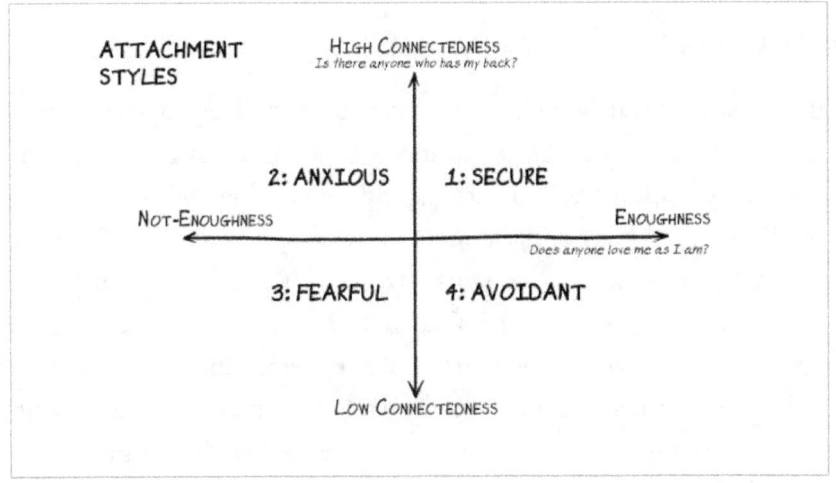

See the Attachment Styles diagram. There are two axes forming a cross. The vertical axis (y-axis), the "connectedness" (or relational) axis, is your midbrain's expectation that relationships are generally good for you or not good for you. Simply, if you find joy, value, identity, and worth mainly through interactions with others, you will be high on this axis. If you have had bad experiences with relationships, they have been a source of hurt, you will be lower on the vertical scale.

The horizontal axis (x-axis) is your inner sense of self-worth ("enoughness"). A positive sense of self-worth (located to the right on the axis) reflects a healthy self-regard that does not require much external validation from outside sources: your partner, other relationships, social media, or success. This scale reflects your internal answer to your unspoken question, "Am I lovable?"

The two axes form four quadrants of attachment styles, proceeding counterclockwise from the upper right quadrant: secure, anxious, fearful, and avoidant, with one quadrant representing secure and three representing insecure attachment.

SECURE ATTACHMENT

If you have a secure attachment style, you would likely describe your-self as having a high sense of connectedness and enoughness. To the internal question, "Are relationships and vulnerability good for you?" your inner working model will tend to answer, "Yes!" To the internal question, "Are you worthy and lovable?" your unspoken answer is "Yes!" You make great partners, resilient in the face of stress, optimistic, curious, empathetic, open to exploring your partner's feelings, and able to regulate your own emotions when stressed out. Counselors love you on their couch. Everything they suggest pays huge dividends.

Unfortunately, most people tend to fall into one of the three insecure attachment styles.

AVOIDANT ATTACHMENT

If you fall in the avoidant attachment style quadrant, you have a posi-tive sense of your self-worth; however, your experience has been that being vulnerable to others in relationships has not been positive and may have even been hurtful. Nothing has hurt you more than rela-tionships gone bad. No judgment.

Perhaps in your childhood, someone close to you let you down or hurt you. Your midbrain did what it was designed to do and created relational protective inner working models to prevent that from happening again. This does not make you broken or bad. You simply are who you are. Being alone is often preferable to being with others.

If you are avoidant, you are likely seen as self-reliant. It's true that you enjoy working alone. Sometimes, you don't feel the need to keep your partner in the loop. You might get stressed out or feel trapped when your significant other wants to have that 'relationship talk' replete with sharing emotions or 'this is how that made me feel' conversations.

Chances are, you have developed a highly sensitive radar warning system alerting you to manipulation, being blamed, or even being criticized. While others are more comfortable sharing emotions and feelings, you thrive in the realm of ideas, concepts, and hypotheticals —and most likely can be a bit passive-aggressive. Do you wonder why arguments need to be so long? Doesn't it make more sense to simply agree to disagree and get back to what you were doing when you were interrupted? If this describes you, you may be avoidant.

ANXIOUS ATTACHMENT

If your attachment style is anxious, your intrinsic sense of self-worth is low, but you find value, identity, and dopamine hits primarily through connections. Most likely, you were subconsciously dissatisfied with the amount of attention you received from one or both parents when you were quite young. You feel intrinsically unworthy of the attention of others. To get rid of that sense of unworthiness and emotionally soothe yourself, you have become quite adept at using and, sometimes, manipulating relationships.

Do you occasionally initiate an argument solely to get your partner to notice you, or have you weaponized the 'this is how you made me feel" conversation? Has anyone identified you as high maintenance because you seem to crave attention from your partner while, at the time, openly worrying about being abandoned, dismissed, or left out? Annie Chen writes, "Being in a relationship with someone who is acting out an anxious attachment style can feel like dealing with an angry customer while staffing a support/complaint desk."[2]

---

2. Chen, A. (2019). The Attachment Theory Workbook: Powerful Tools to Promote Understanding, Increase Stability, and Build Lasting Relationships. Althea Press. p. 28

FEARFUL ATTACHMENT

The last category is the smallest of the four—and that's a good thing. The person in this category is experiencing a subconscious sense of not-enoughness as well as a fear of disconnectedness—a hybrid combination of anxious and avoidant attachment concerns. Their brains' wiring tends to make them want to urgently avoid vulnerability and openness out of fear of possible rejection. They may vacillate between longing and fear, demanding connection and then distancing themselves from it—and may even lash out when a connection is offered or may emotionally shut down. It can be common with adults who have some history of trauma, abuse, and neglect, particularly as infants.

No matter which major insecure attachment style you find yourself in, you are not broken. God loves you as much as the Father loves the Son, and the Son loves the Father. He does not love secure partners more. However, it is easy to see how relationships can become cross-wired quickly—and neither partner has any idea what happened.

Consider the possible relational struggles that might erupt if an extremely avoidant and an extremely anxious attachment style got together. Or two avoidants. Or two anxious. For any combination, Paul would admonish you to stop trying to adjust and work it out on your own. You need heavenly intervention.

If you want to know what your or your partner's attachment style is, we provide a helpful survey in my Good Enough Parent program (www.goodenoughparent.online). Here is a short version for your benefit.

Mark the paragraph with which you most identify.

1. *"I am somewhat uncomfortable being close to others. I find it difficult to trust them completely and difficult to allow myself to depend on them. I am nervous when anyone gets*

*too close, and often, others want me to be more intimate
than I feel comfortable being."*

2. *"I find it relatively easy to get close to others and am
comfortable depending on them and having them depend
on me. I don't worry about being abandoned or about
someone getting too close to me."*

3. *"I find others are reluctant to get as close as I would like. I
often worry that my partner doesn't really love me or won't
want to stay with me. I want to get very close to my partner,
and this sometimes scares them away."*

4. *"I am somewhat uncomfortable getting close to others. I
want emotionally close relationships, but I find it difficult
to trust others completely or to depend on them. I sometimes
worry I will be hurt if I allow myself to become too close to
others."*

Did you pick one? Label paragraph #1: Avoidant. Paragraph #2: Secure. Paragraph #3: Anxious. Paragraph #4: Fearful. These options are not evil by any means. They are very human and largely reflect your previous experiences with faulty—sometimes scary and harmful relationships.

Let's delve back into the Gospel App Shape.

ADDICTION

The fourth internalized power that drags Samantha down is *addiction*.

Addictions are the people, places, and things we turn to to escape the pain, fear, and remorse rooted in the three deeper emotional forces: guilt, shame, and insecurity. They are often fueled by negative core beliefs that keep us trapped in a cycle of avoidance and self-sabotage.

"I am powerless."

"I am incomplete."

"I have no influence on this got-to-have-now power."

"I can't control my brain. I can't stop."

"I can't go in a different direction."

"I am empty, thirsty, and incomplete."

"Nothing satisfies. Nothing fills."

Here's Pastor and theologian Tim Keller.

> "You know how addiction works. It starts like this: There's some kind of disappointment or distress in your life. As a result, you choose to deal with that distress with an agent; it might be sex, it might be drugs, it might be alcohol. The agent promises transcendence. The agent promises freedom, a sense of being in control, a sense of being above all this, a sense of being liberated, a sense of escape. And so, you do it. But when you do it, when you take the addicting agent as a way of dealing with life, the trap is set."[3]

Is it any wonder why you might subconsciously launch into your fingerprint under-the-curve reactionary behaviors? It's no wonder that others do the same. Doesn't this explain a lot of your conflicts and struggles? This doesn't absolve anyone of consequences—not at all.

---

3. "Sin As Slavery," Gospel In Life, Tim Keller, March 17, 1996, https://gospelinlife. com/sermon/sin-as-slavery/

ACCESSING GOD'S POWER: THE SIMPLE UNCLUTTERED GOSPEL

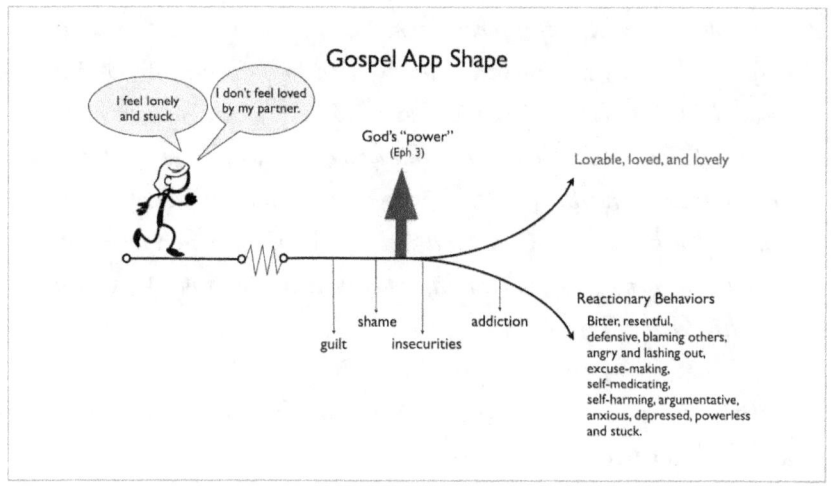

Now look at the new Gospel App Shape in your book. There is an added upward arrow, **God's Power** that works directly opposite the four downward powers. Instead of letting the four downward powers keep Samantha (or Jamal) stuck in that endless cycle of reactionary behaviors, she can take Paul's teaching seriously and ask for God's power to fight back against the powers of guilt, shame, insecurities, and addiction. It is that simple. She can let power fight power. Empowered by God, she can begin to experience being lovable, loved and lovely.

PRE-COUCH EXERCISE:

How? Keep saying the Simple Uncluttered Gospel to your midbrain twice a day for forty-five days. Say it word for word. Repetition is important. Say it aloud. Here it is.

"Jesus-Follower, strictly because of what Jesus did for you 2000 years ago, God actually loves you. He loves you with all His heart, as much

as the Father loves the Son and the Son loves the Father. He can't love you any more or any less than He does right now—even if you were a better partner. He loves you as you are, not as you should be or could be. You can't add to this love or take away from it. Now I get it, it often feels like you've messed it up, or need to do something so God would like you better. Not so. How do you experience it more now? Simple! Good news, there is something you can do and are invited to do. You can take daily baby steps to ask the Spirit inside of you to make you know, experience, and feel just how much God loves you right now. Just ask. Ask again later today. Ask tomorrow. Make it a spiritual habit."

What jumped off the page? What hadn't you thought about before? What causes you concern?

Here's the rub. No judgment, but because of your subconscious intrinsic shame, guilt, insecurities, and addictions, you may have a hard time looking up into the face of Jesus and asking him to intervene with His power. It's not all your fault, and you're not alone. I suspect, though, that in your honest moments, you know you can't keep doing what you're doing. We created the Simple Uncluttered Gospel for real people like you. Say it twice a day for forty-five days. You can do that.

In his first public message, Jesus said some radical, unbelievable things. You can see his words in Luke 4:18-19. I have taken the liberty to expand His words in a way that speaks to the Samanthas and Jamals of the world. Enjoy.

"I am the one powerfully filled by God's very Spirit. Yahweh Himself charged me to proclaim the good news at last to the poorest and most ashamed in the land. Samantha and Jamal, when was the last time you heard good news?

Yahweh sent me a life-changing message for you who feel like a prisoner in your relationship. Be free! There are a lot of different kinds of incarceration and slavery. I say, 'Come to me and feel true freedom in your current relations.'

My charge includes telling the blind, you who feel like an untouchable here, an outcast, unwelcomed, you who feel like you must beg for love, I say in the name of my Father, 'See!' There are many kinds of blindness. Am I right? It is time to *see* beyond your current circle of despair and envision something new and miraculous—to see hope at last.

Also, I have come to pursue you who carry shame, who feel like you have little worth in your partner's eyes. Not only will I pursue you, but I will raise you to places of honor and worth. Won't that be something when it happens?

One last thing. I have come to tell you who fear you have disappointed God; do not believe the lie. God innately loves sinners; that's all there is. He perfectly loves the unlovable, the unloved, and the unlovely, and that's all of us on any given day. In my power, you will hear God say, 'You are my beloved son or daughter with whom I am well pleased.' I will make that happen."

— LK 4:18-19 (HIGHLY REVISED)

HOMEWORK:

- Go to the online course Good Enough Parent (www. goodenoughparent.online), and begin to go through it even if you do not have children. The material on the Attachment Theory and attunement is worth the price of admission. Oh, by the way, it's free.

- Google "From Now On" by Flatirons Community Church and let it pour over you.

QUESTIONS FOR PARTNERS TO CONSIDER

1. What did you hear that was new to you? Helpful?
2. Do you resonate with the concept of powerlessness? Unpack that. What has seemed to work for you when you feel powerless?
3. What resonated with you as you read the Simple Uncluttered Gospel this time?
4. Which attachment style did you most resonate with? Remember, it is not a question of good or bad or right or wrong. Do you have a story that points in one of the directions?

7

TIP #6: YOU HAVE DADDY ISSUES

ACCEPT IT—IT'S NOT ALL YOUR FAULT.

"The relationship with our fathers creates the filter with which we view ourselves and those we love. It colours our relationships with others and influences important decisions we make in our lives such as who we are, our life goals, and our deep values."

— ELISABETTA FRANZOSO

"Every week wounded women come into my office suffering from a poor self-image, from the inability to form lasting relationships, or from a lack of confidence in their ability to work and function in the world. On the surface these women often appear quite successful...but underneath the veneer of success or contentment is the injured self, the hidden despair, the feelings of loneliness and isolation, the fear of abandonment and rejection, the tears and the rage. For many of these women, the root of their injury stems from a damaged relationship with the father."

— LINDA SCHIERSE

We all have father issues, both women and men.

WHEN WE LEGITIMATELY FEEL LONELY, unappreciated, disrespected, unloved, insecure, or dishonored, it's easy to blame our partner—all of us have at one time or another. But these feelings are not all our fault. Recognizing that this isn't just about your partner is actually good news for you and your relationship.

It's possible to understand that much of this pain originates from something more profound than your current relationship with your partner—and still hold yourself and your partner accountable for the work that needs to be done. Neither love languages nor any other creative to-dos will quell these deeply rooted, subconscious feelings.

If your father was emotionally distant, abusive, or inconsistent in his connection with you starting from the third trimester of pregnancy onward, you likely carry a residual and unconscious fear of abandonment. This fear will, to one degree or another, make it harder for you to trust relationships. Think of it as an underlying nagging suspicion of partners.

And here's the important part: This is not entirely your fault, nor is it fully your partner's fault.

The reality is that *all* of us have such "daddy issues"—whether we want to acknowledge them or not. No one escapes unscathed. Acknowledging this possibility can be uncomfortable, but this should be comforting news for all struggling relationships.

DADDY ISSUES

Unfortunately, the term "daddy issues" has been trivialized, especially in modern discourse. It has become a catchphrase for women seen as overly sexual or emotionally unstable because of their negative experiences with their fathers. This stereotype leads to a narrow and damaging understanding of what "daddy issues" really are. It's far more complex and affects both men and women.

Initially, the term "Father Complex" was a clinical concept used to describe the damaging effects of toxic father-son relationships. As psychologists explored the dynamics further, they realized these unresolved issues had a significant impact on both men and women.

IT'S BIGGER THAN THAT

Our subconscious wounds extend beyond our relationship with our all-too-human *paterfamilias*.

God created us to long for 'Father' in a deeper, more universal sense beyond our physical father. 'Father experience' is the state where we feel enough, worthy, secure, lovable, and lovely. In the father-embrace, we are finally exposed to a profound sense of being cherished and feel appreciated for who we are. In this place, we no longer feel lonely or abandoned because, somehow, we are aware we are loved, even in our most vulnerable state.

This longing for father is part of our core DNA. It is how God created us. Our human relationships, no matter how good, can *never* fully replace what we were designed to find in the arms of our Heavenly Father.

When hurting couples come for counseling, it's common for one or both partners to focus on the other, blaming them for legitimate feelings of being overlooked, abandoned, lonely, or unloved. These emotions are deeply valid and real. However, a larger culprit is lurking in the unseeable shadows of their midbrains—a deeper, more primal issue that is often overlooked and not fully acknowledged.

Your partner can't satisfy your deepest father-longings.

They do not have the capacity. Even if you and your partner were truly consistent with love languages and heroically gave each other the '5 A's of Love' (attention, acceptance, appreciation, affection, and allowing), at a certain level, your midbrain longs for even more.

It is not all your or your partner's fault.

It is not Dr. Chapman's fault.

In a higher sense, you and your partner are each on a quest, ordained by God, to find Father. Here's how I described it in my fourth Kingdom Quest Christian fantasy book for young readers (ages 10-16), *The Tale of the Orphan Magician*. Rahgornah, the dragon storyteller, begins the tale.

> *"At the heart of every powerful, lasting tale and at the center of all reliable history is a single obsessive, though often subconscious, quest. I am speaking of the single driving theme of every reliable tale ever told. One of our esteemed Sakalon elders rightly referred to it as a 'search for father.' This is not just a search for a male progenitor, or yours or my paterfamilias, but something weightier and more elusive at times. Many of us have suffered from poor or absent fathers. I do not mean to say we long for an individual. No, we long for the experience of father...Though we are very different in so many ways, humans, elves, trolls, dwarves, each of us—at our core—longs for 'father'—and will never be satisfied until we arrive in that father embrace."*

Here's my point. No matter how good your physical father was or how loving your partner is, they cannot satisfy your voracious, innate, God-designed human need for Father. None of us, male or female, this side of glory will feel satisfied or fully 'fathered'—and so, the quest.

This should be good news for some who experienced poor relationships with their human father. No matter how bad or absent your father was, you can still experience 'Father' now.

Here's Rahgornah again.

"When I say that we all long for father, I am not speaking about a person or a creature. I am speaking of a place, an embrace, a relationship where you can hear and experience the phrase, 'You are my beloved child with whom I am so pleased.' In that hug, you feel absolutely lovable to that person, and you can rest knowing, whoever or whatever they are, they have your back if something bad happens to you or you do something wrong...This is particularly true since the Great Rebellion."

Rahgornah continues.

"Since the Great Rebellion, each of us individuals, tribes and countries are emotional and relational orphans longing for father. All creatures, male, female, or asexual, long to experience that worthiness in the eyes of 'other.'" He used air quotes with his talons.

"In a word, enoughness. Am I beautiful, handsome, attractive, desirable enough, worthy of honor and attention of those who are important to me? Simply, am I lovable enough? Just hearing some kind person saying it is not sufficient. We need to experience enoughness regularly, or we will begin to forcefully take it from each other."

THE BEGINNING OF DADDY ISSUES

Biblically, where did these daddy issues originate? It is safe to suggest that even though they did not have a physical father, neither Adam nor Eve had any daddy issues. Their innate longing for that experience of Father was fully satisfied daily by their interactions with their heavenly Father Himself.

How would experiencing Father regularly affect me, my sense of identity, or my relationships with others? It is worth the time to ponder, but honestly, it is like asking a blind person to imagine 'blue' or a turtle how to fly.

THE FALL: SEPARATION FROM FATHER

When Adam and Eve ate from the tree in the middle of the garden, it marked a profound shift in the human experience—one that is often referred to as the *Fall*.

The key to understanding the tragedy of the Fall lies in the loss of something far more acute than a break in obedience: Adam and Eve lost the experience of *Father* that they had enjoyed since their inception.

Let me be clear: God did not remove the Father-experience from them as punishment. Instead, it was *they* who could no longer experience Father. Let's look at this passage closely.

> *"When the woman saw that the fruit of the tree was good for food and pleasing to the eye, and also desirable for gaining wisdom, she took some and ate it. She also gave some to her husband, who was with her, and he ate it. Then the eyes of both of them were opened, and they realized they were naked...Then the man and his wife heard the sound of the Lord God as He was walking in the garden in the cool of the day, and they hid from the Lord God among the trees of the garden. But the Lord God called to the man, 'Where are you?'"*

> — GEN 3:6-9

THE TRAGEDY: THE FIRST BARRIER TO FATHER

At first, everything seemed the same. God as Father was still right there walking in the garden, calling for His children, inviting them into dialogue, inviting them to Father. Though the source of Father was not gone, for the first time in human history, their capacity to *experience* Father was crippled. In a nanosecond, their brains did what they were created to do when fear, shame, and guilt struck. It developed a protective barrier blocking the first couple's capacity to experience Father.

The first sin caused a profound internal shift in their psyches. It seemed they could no longer look up into God's eyes and experience the Father-love for which they were created. Instead, they were filled with shame, fear, and insecurity—emotions they had never known before—and today, we are well familiar with them.

We have since labeled this condition Original Sin—
a brokenness that affects not only our legal standing before
God but also our ability to receive and experience Father.

Since then, every human being on the planet, with one exception, has been born with a Father gap in their psyches and heavily fortified midbrains designed to protect them from pain and hurt, which ironically hinders them from experiencing the Father-embrace. At the same time, all humanity is desperately looking for Father in all the wrong places—and ironically, remains resistant to ever finding Father.

THE FIRST APPEARANCE OF THE ABSENCE OF FATHER

When Adam and Eve ate the fruit, they experienced a profound brain rewiring. God had not withdrawn. Adam and Eve, who once would enthusiastically run to God at the sound of His footsteps, now *hid* from Him in fear.

"Adam answered, 'I heard you in the garden, and I was afraid because I was naked; so, I hid.' And he said, 'Who told you that you were naked? Have you eaten from the tree that I commanded you not to eat from?' The man said, 'The woman you put here with me—she gave me some fruit from the tree, and I ate it.' Then the Lord God

said to the woman, 'What is this you have done?' The woman said,
'The serpent deceived me, and I ate.'"

Notice the rapid shift in their behavior. This was the birth of human individualism—where self-preservation and blame-shifting became our default modes of operation. It was the first time partners blamed each other for their own feelings of shame, exposure, and loneliness. It would not be the last.

This also marked the beginning of the broken human condition and served as a harbinger of all the relational difficulties yet to come. Whether we realize it or not, all men and women are now born in a state of Father-deprivation.

THE UNMET NEED FOR FATHER IN OUR RELATIONSHIPS

This is perhaps the most significant reason why all relationships, at their core, can be so difficult. In one way or another, we are all subconsciously trying to fix what was broken in the garden—trying to get back to the experience of Father that was fragmented in Adam and Eve's fall. Here's *The Tale of the Orphan Magician* again.

"All history is a repetitive bite of the poisonous fruit that led to the Great Rebellion but also unleashed an epidemic of the lack of enoughness—leading to the Trollian Wars, the Great Buzite War and even that last little argument you had with your partner today.

"In one sense, it is not all your fault. Of course, you are responsible for your choices. But unbeknownst to you, there has been a real power inside of you, a vile, unslain dragon that is driving you to fight for the limited enoughness available in this enoughness-challenged world. That searching and not finding ultimately ends with the

haves and the have-nots and all subsequent disagreements, hoarding,
robberies and wars. But ultimately, your brain will never rest until
you find father again."

So, why did God curse the first couple and banish them from the Garden with the implication of being away from 'father?' The story of Cain and Abel will give us more clues and help us understand what was really happening then—and today in our relationships.

CAIN (HEBREW 'QAYEEN') AND ABEL (HEBREW 'HEVEL')

Qayeen and Hevel's story (Gen 4) brings us face-to-face with the deeper, often-overlooked layers of human psychology, divine love, and the intricate dynamics of our relationship with God as Father. Let us unpack it.

At first glance, Qayeen and Hevel's offerings seem like a simple matter of the first two sons trying to access the experience of 'Father' that their parents had abandoned. We have no record that God required offerings at that time to earn or prove oneself worthy of His favor. I suspect the two boys were endeavoring to find Father, with very little information on how to do it.

You know the story. The way we typically describe the account, God accepted Hevel's offering and rejected Qayeen's. In Genesis 4:4, the Hebrew text states that God gazed at, regarded, and paid attention to Hevel (and his offering) but paid no attention to Qayeen (and his offering). The implication is that Hevel experienced Father, while the firstborn did not. The plot thickens.

What might God be thinking? It's always dangerous to speculate. But this seems like a straightforward story of 'doing right' versus 'doing wrong'—a tale of God preferring the better offering from Hevel, the shepherd, who brought the best of his flock—his firstborn sheep—while Qayeen, the farmer, offered *some* of his crops.

79

This interpretation doesn't quite capture the deeper issue at play.

Qayeen's offering of crops would have been considered perfectly acceptable under later Jewish law (Lev. 2:1-2). As for Hevel's offering, while it seems commendable at first glance, it falls short by later standards as well (Ex. 13:11-12) since he only offered *some* of the firstborn, not all. So, we can't attribute God's favor to the offerings themselves, at least not in the way we typically think.

QUEST FOR FATHER

I propose that God took this opportunity to shape a surprising, mysterious quest for the unsuspecting firstborn son of Adam and Eve. It was a stunning act of great favor and a subtle invitation to a journey where, in the end, Qayeen would experience Father. Surely, Qayeen didn't see it that way. Instead, the disrespect he felt incited his brain to rage.

> *"So Qayeen was very angry, and his face was downcast. Then the Lord said to Qayeen, 'If you do what is right, will you not be accepted? But if you do not do what is right, sin is crouching at your door; it desires to have you, but you must master it.'"*

> — GEN 4:6-7

'Downcast' doesn't just describe the physical act of looking down; it represents an emotional withdrawal. Qayeen would not—could not—look up into God's face. He was unable or unwilling to meet the Father who was so close and, I suggest, was ready to embrace him.

The Hebrew word most often translated as 'accepted' is better translated as 'to raise up,' likely referring to his downcast face. Here is a legit interpretive unpacking of the account.

"Qayeen was incited with anger, and his eyes were downcast, unable or unwilling to look at God in the face. Then the Lord said to Qayeen. 'Why are you angry? Why won't you do right and look into my eyes and experience *Father*? If you do not, you will inevitably go down a very selfish and destructive path and be unable to stop it."[1]

God's response to Qayeen is not one of anger or wrath (as many might expect). Instead, God asks a gentle, probing question: "Why are you angry? Why do you look down instead of looking up into My eyes?" Qayeen's God-ordained quest was to do what was right and enter the Father embrace, as he is, with empty hands. No offering required.

This is the heart of the Father for all of us Qayeens.
He desires that we experience His love and favor,
fully aware we have done nothing to earn it.
We do not enter the Father's love because we are worthy.
It is the Father's embrace that makes us worthy.

---

1. Theologian John Calvin concurs that this is a very difficult passage to interpret and has led to much dialogue. "Some of the Hebrew Doctors refer it [the Hebrew word most often translated 'accepted'] to the countenance of Cain, as if God promised that he would lift it up though now cast down with sorrow." The idea is that Cain would not look up into God's eyes due to his anger and perceived disrespect. God could be saying that the best thing for him to do would be to look up and finally experience the favor that he longed for from the beginning (i.e., the reason for the offering), or perhaps God will cause that to happen. Either way, if Cain doesn't experience the favor from God in that moment, God is telling him that he will not be able to stop what was coming. Of course, Cain did not look up and Abel was murdered.

RESULT OF NOT RECEIVING FATHER?

"Now Qayeen said to his brother Hevel, 'Let's go out to the field.' And while they were in the field, Qayeen attacked his brother Hevel and killed him."

— GEN 4:8

Qayeen's murder of Hevel is the ultimate act of reaction, not reason. This is what people who are unable to grasp 'Father' subconsciously tend to do. They can't help it. Qayeen reacts out of a frustrated vacuum of Father rather than a soul loved by Father.

What is particularly striking is that even in the aftermath of this terrible act, God doesn't respond with the expected wrath. Instead, He asks Qayeen, "Where is your brother Hevel?"

God is not asking out of ignorance—He knows precisely what Qayeen has done. I suggest that God is trying to help Qayeen confront his own lack of Father. The Qayeen quest is not over. He is given another unlikely opportunity to find Father, even after a horrific crime. But instead, Qayeen responds with defensiveness and anxiety: "Am I my brother's keeper?" He is not acting as a person filled with the fullness of Father (Eph 3). It sounds remarkably similar to my reaction to a recent argument. You too?

His ordained quest for Father is still not complete. Almost every quest goes downhill before it goes up. God punishes Qayeen (Gen 4:12). Yet in the punishment, we see something unexpected. The curses are severe but hardly final. Qayeen will no longer be able to find rest in the land. The earth, which once yielded crops for him, will now be uncooperative. He will wander, restless, disconnected from the world and God.

Let me ask. Do you read into the narrative that this is it? God is done? Qayeen got what he deserved, so let's move on to the next story. That may be how you feel about your relationship, too. I suggest God is not done with Qayeen yet.

God's curse is not a sentence of death. Despite the gravity of his crime, the Father's arms are yet open wide. He marks Qayeen with a sign to protect him from being killed by others. This is an act of Father-mercy—a safeguard to prevent the rebellious murderer Qayeen from being struck down by others who might seek revenge. Even in his darkest moment, Qayeen is shown a remaining pathway to Father love that he does not deserve and hasn't earned.

There is some evidence that the quest is beginning to bear its first fruit. See the little phrase of Qayeen, "And I will be hidden from your presence." (Gen 4:14) First, God never says that at all. You could translate Qayeen's complaint, "I can never enter Father-embrace then." God does not say that.

God's end game remains. Qayeen can still look up to see God's favorable gaze and be restored to the Father experience that his parents abandoned. Qayeen still won't look up. Ironically, he blames God for not being able to do so. But are we at the end of the story?

Here's how the Great King (God) describes it in *The Tale of the Orphan Magician*.

"'So, King Hamedan and Prime Minister Eiren, your mutual fore-father, Qayeen, desperately wanted to experience the delight of father, but he refused it when it was offered. Why? Lots of reasons, no doubt. His mind was poisoned by a toxic combination of shame, guilt and rage. He wasn't thinking rationally. When I graciously held out my hand and offered him forgiveness, favor, and restored honor, a nasty dragon inside his brain—which we all have to one degree or another, deceived him. At that moment, he wouldn't—he couldn't.'

"'So, he ran away to this new continent, not to make a home, but to run away from one. The absence of father delight was passed down from parent to child, to grandchild, and so on, generation after

generation in Amaratzim. This metastasized into broken families,
rage, polarization, tribalism, conquest, genocide and more. Need we
look any further than Qayeen's own sons?'

"'But why didn't you force Qayeen to accept your offer?' barked the
corpulent Hamedan at the Great King.

"'That is not how this works,' replied the King with eyes furrowed.
'The prodigal must willingly enter the father's delight. At the time,
Qayeen was unwilling and too ashamed, you see? So, without telling
Qayeen, I created a quest for him, a great quest suitable for a knight
of character, substance and potential greatness. What was the quest?
He was to go and find father. Though he never caught on that it was
I who so be'd such a quest, he enthusiastically went out to find father
on his own—just never did—not yet. Hamedan and his descendants
remain on that quest. Truly great quests can take years, decades, or,
in this case, generations.

This story only makes sense if, like the Father of the Prodigal in
Jesus' parable, God the Father is furiously pursuing his lost son. All
Qayeen ever had to do, like his parents before him, was to "do what is
right" and look up into the Father's eyes. Qayeen's Father-ordained
quest, a strange and wonderful favor extended by God to the firstborn, was to undo the damaged relationship caused by his parents'
bite of the fruit.

Until Qayeen experiences Father, he will remain insecure in all
his relationships—every one of them. He will never be who he could
be. He can only be Qayeen-lite, lonely, guilty, ashamed, paranoid
(they will kill me), acting out to punish God, the very one he initially
sought favor from—all the things you and I suffer from daily if we
are honest.

The Qayeen and Hevel account wasn't a morality lesson on the benefits of good offerings. It is the first (of many) God-ordained quests for an emotional orphan to find Father at last.

Wouldn't that have been far better than an *at-a-boy* for bringing a good offering?

I like how theologian Don Hudson puts such God-ordained quests in an insightful article, *Searching for Our Fathers.*

> *"It is when we are fatherless that we quest for father...If the father is with us, we have no need of him. It seems to be that only when the father...is gone that we search for him...The father leaves or we leave the father. This is the first stage of the journey. In many ways, one's story does not begin until the father is out of the immediate picture. Otherwise, we would just hang around the house and do what is necessary. We would bask in the father's presence. We would never be lost. We would not know sin. We would not know redemption. Ironically, we would not seek to know the father. The father's absence cast us out of the garden and into the journey."*[2]

In summary, this is God's stunning DNA. He innately pursues father-deficient sons and daughters as they are. His embrace is for empty sinners.

PRACTICAL APPLICATION FOR COUPLES

I mentioned earlier that recognizing father issues is good news for troubled couples. Let me explain. Like Adam, Eve, and Qayeen before you, you are on a divinely ordained quest to find Father. Amid your current relational struggles, imagine shedding the mask of Qayeen. You are not experiencing Father as you should or could, but

---

2. Hudson, Don, Searching for Our Fathers, Mars Hill Review, Winter/Spring, 1998, p. 39-42.

you are invited to look up and find a better Father experience than you've felt in your relationships with faulty humans.

Blaming your partner may be partly true, but it won't scratch your deeper Father-itch. You are in a place where you have lost Father. That is motivational. Here's Hudson again.

> "Though God is not the author of evil, he is a Father who invites his children to the journey—the journey of redemption, the journey of knowing the Father's heart. There is something respectful about God's silence at the temptation. He invites his children to choose, to fail, to sin, to be redeemed. In essence, he invites them to the journey...The search begins in the absence of God...In the Old Testament, to repent is to return. The Hebrew word is shuv—'to return.' As a result of the Fall, we all hide our faces from one another and from God. To sin is to turn our face away from the Father, to be in exile with the mark of Qayeen. To return is to bring our face back to the Father. If we forge ahead without the Father, we will continue to be lost children wandering in exile. If we bring our faces back to him—which is what our hearts desire—then we will find the one we have been searching for...The subtle beauty of the story of the prodigal son is the 'moving toward' of both father and son. There really is somewhere to go in the most confounding moments of life. The father is looking for the child; the child must only return. Revelry awaits the return of the child."[3]

---

3. Ibid, *Searching*, p. 47. *"The hiddenness of God is also one of the neglected truths of American pop-oriented Christianity...When we pretend that the father is always with us, we become the older brother of the prodigal son, and we stay home and take care of the farm. We learn obedience but we never learn forgiveness. We learn what the father demands, but we never get to know the father's heart. We learn to be content, but we never lose our heats to desire...'...[T]o not have is the beginning of desire,' said Wallace Stevens. Absence evokes presence. Silence rouses language. Hate begs for love. Hunger demands fulfillment. Losing the father constrains us to yearn for father. Would we ever search for the father if he were always with us? Losing the father puts us on the path of searching for the father....Though God is not the author of evil, he is a Father who invites his children to the journey—the journey of redemption, the journey of knowing the Father's heart. There*

Imagine God standing before you and asking.

"Why are you frustrated and defeated, strangled by far too many subconscious daddy issues being manifested in your relationships now? Why do you blame your partner? They are on their own quest to find Me. Will you look me in the face? In my eyes? Will you find Father now from me? Have you begun to see that your partner can't be that source? Will you look up? Or, if you can't, will you ask me to *make* your eyes look up?"

Imagine how the Qayeen story would have ended differently if he had looked up and received the experienced favor that he longed for in the eyes of God.

Imagine the difference it could make in your feeling of enoughness, being lovable, loved, and lovely. Imagine the difference it might make if your partner grasped Father as well. How about your relationship? I believe that the use of love languages would only then multiply in value and worth.

PRAY

Jesus-follower, how do you access Father? All you need to do is, by faith, through the power of the Holy Spirit, ask. Check out the Qayeen Prayer.

"God, I am beginning to see I am afraid of trusting You. Trusting has not been good for me—betrayal, broken trust—all too painful. In my head, I want to look up and see into Your eyes. Yet I am scared to death of what I may see. I can't. I won't. I need Your power to enable

---

is something respectful about God's silence at the temptation. He invites his children to choose, to fail, to sin, to be redeemed. In essence, he invites them to the journey...The search begins in the absence of God." (42-7) me to look up—to want to look up. To be honest, I wonder if You would ever say to me, 'This is my beloved son or daughter, with whom I am well pleased.' I want to hear You say it. I want to believe it is true. In my brain, I know Jesus purchased it for me. I have a hard time believing it in my soul. I desperately want to hear You say it to me. Make me believe it is so. I need to feel the honor of being a child of Yours in good standing. I have endured great dishonor and disrespect here. Make me receive the honor of adoption that Jesus paid so dearly for. Now, please. I am weary of all the games I am playing. I am tired of being lonely, being afraid, blaming You, my partner, myself, and others, wearing masks, acting out, and holding up boundaries to protect my heart. Spirit, quick, give me power to look up and experience Father."

EXTRA EFFORT: FATHER-ISSUE SURVEY

If you want to delve a bit deeper and explore the fingerprints of father issues in your life and relationships, consider taking the following non-scientific survey. You can be honest. It is designed to measure how 'fatherless' you are at this moment. **Remember, it is not all your fault**. If you are willing, have someone you trust to speak the truth take the survey on your behalf. (Scoring: 0-Not my experience. 1-Not sure, maybe a little. 2-Okay, some. 3-More than I want to admit. 4-A lot.

1. As a child, I didn't get the desired affection from my father, or he was emotionally unavailable or worse—and to one degree or another, I still defend him.
2. I constantly need verbal, emotional, or physical validation from others in my life, men and women, children, friends, colleagues, and even strangers.
3. I tend to gravitate toward others with daddy issues—the end of which is usually a train-wreck.

4. My spouse/partner complains that I cannot handle criticism.
5. I fear being alone. Having to be by myself with no one to interact with makes me uneasy, anxious, or depressed.
6. I can't trust others, unconsciously assuming they have hidden motives, will fail me, or have bad intentions. I am suspicious that all interactions have strings attached.
7. Compromise is a four-letter word to me.
8. I complain that my partner/spouse appreciates and validates their colleagues and friends more than me.
9. I can't feel confident my spouse or partner will support me during tough times. I fear ultimately finding myself abandoned, alone, and vulnerable.
10. I can't be on my own and find myself subconsciously needing more and longer 'facetime' with others (social media, conversations, gatherings).
11. A significant part of my self-worth and feeling good about myself is tied to how I think others feel about me —good or bad.
12. I feel left out when my spouse/partner makes plans without me.
13. I can't forgive.
14. I need to be constantly productive, and my worth is tied to the service or product I provide.
15. FOMO is a real thing for me. I can't take being left out of some activity, unaware of a joke, or uninvited.
16. When I read-between-the-lines of a conversation (which I will always tend to do), I generally think the worst.
17. I overkill projects I take on because, in the end, I fear criticism for a bad or flawed job, but even more, I need recognition and praise from others—I never feel I did well enough.

18. I can't trust that my spouse/partner has my best interests at heart.
19. I have great difficulty admitting being wrong or making a mistake for fear of being rejected or abandoned. When I do admit it, it feels shallow and self-justifying to my partner/spouse.
20. My spouse/partner complains that I am critical, nagging, blaming, back-seat driving, micro-managing, or demeaning.
21. My mind often fixates on potential conflicts or lack of relationships, making it hard for me to enjoy the present, feel less worried, or more hopeful.
22. I must second guess everything.
23. I need constant affirmation from my spouse/partner, but it doesn't seem to help how I feel.
24. I can't stand being labeled as having daddy issues.
25. It's my partner/spouse's fault.

> *0-25: Congratulations, you are a remarkable, unusually secure human being living between the Fall and Heaven.*
>
> *26+: Great news, beloved of God. You are, to one degree or another, a functioning orphan with noticeable daddy issues on that same glorious quest as Qayeen before you. It is not all your or your spouse/partner's fault. You will be surprised at what can happen as you begin to ask God to make you experience his embrace. This is your God-ordained quest. Access Father now.*

QUESTIONS FOR PARTNERS TO CONSIDER

1. What did you hear that was new to you? Helpful?
   Explain.
2. When you heard the author say that you have daddy
   issues, how did you feel? What was your immediate knee-
   jerk reaction? Explain.
3. The Qayeen Prayer is mainly about 'trust'—or the lack of
   trust. How does that sync with daddy issues? How does
   that sync with your current struggles? Again, there is no
   judgment.
4. Did this chapter just weird you out? Explain.
5. Are you still wondering when we'll get to the good stuff,
   like what my partner should be doing differently?
   Unpack. No judgment.

8

TIP #7: YOU WERE RIGHT ALL ALONG, YOU CAN'T FORGIVE

(AND IT'S NOT ALL YOUR FAULT)

"Forgive you?... Sure, I'll forgive you...The moment I see something I really want on the Shopping Channel.

— EDGAR ARGO

A man is shopping for a card for his wife. "Excuse me, do you have a card that stops short of saying 'I'm sorry' yet vaguely hints of some wrongdoing?"

— UNKNOWN

IT'S A BAD NEWS, good news situation. God wisely designed our human brain to protect us from danger. You put your hand on a hot stove and quickly learn not to do that again. The bad news is that your brain's design makes it virtually impossible to forgive all those old hurts, betrayals, disappointments, abuses, lies, and disrespect, private and public—not only from your partner's hurtful behaviors or comments but also from former partners, your parents, and others. It wants to protect you from experiencing that pain again.

Yet, you know you *should* forgive; Jesus said so. But your brain's *hippocampus* stores all that garbage along with the very emotions you felt when those things happened to you. All piled high in a dark—apparently—very accessible corridor of your brain. That is why you get triggered at times. It's all still there.

Imagine your vulnerable, emotional self hunkered down behind well-fortified walls with armed soldiers and advanced weaponry strategically situated all along the top battlement.

Your brain says, "You're welcome!" Those emotional and relational fortifications are designed to protect you from being hurt again. Our brains do this very well and extremely efficiently.

Unfortunately, these walls are great buzzkills for any genuine, intimate, ongoing, or new relationships. They make it virtually impossible to forgive. That makes sense, right?

In our metaphor, to forgive is equivalent to tearing down those inner psychological walls. How is that accomplished? What neural wrecking ball is available? You see the predicament, right?

To think that you can just rationally 'choose' to forgive seems a bit naïve—ultimately doomed to fail.

But didn't Jesus command us to forgive? Yes, but note that he never says how. In the passage in Matthew 18, he tells of a wicked servant who had been forgiven a king's fortune by an over-the-top gracious king. The king wrote himself a check from his own bank account for the debt owed by the foolish, boneheaded servant. If anyone should have been able to forgive a tiny little debt owed him, it would have been the forgiven servant, empowered by gratefulness for the King's grace. But he didn't. That's Jesus' point. We *should* forgive, but we won't. In fact, we can't.

So, what's the next step? I invite you to bring one instance where you have struggled to forgive, old or new, big or small, to my online, confidential spiritual journey, *The Forgiving Path* (www.forgivingpath.com). In under three hours, you will get answers to the question, "Well then, what am I supposed to do?" There is good news. (Use promo code "precouch" to sign up at a significant discount.)

Here's a teaser. When you finally get to heaven, you will notice several things. One of the most amazing things will be that the complicated fortress will be gone, removed by God himself, without you doing a thing. For the first time since the doctor spanked you at birth, you will be grudge-free, shame-free, anger-free, and defensive-ness-free. Try to imagine it. I don't think we can. It would be like us trying to imagine what it would be like to live without gravity. We will look around and say, "Hey, wait a minute, I think I have just forgiven that person."

Good news, child of God. Though *you* can't forgive (because your brain is working against you), God can make you begin to forgive with a wave of his tiny little finger.

So, even if you don't do *The Forgiving Path*, at the very least, do this: ask God to give you <u>*His*</u> forgiveness for that hurt, wound, or crime that is hindering you—protecting you—keeping you from vulnerably loving your partner the way God loves them, or from fully receiving your partner's love for you.

Ask God, like the magnanimous king in Jesus' parable, to write the justice check to cover the debt owed you from His bank account —to fill your emptied cup with the miraculous life-changing fullness of God (Eph 3). Ask for a tiny foretaste of what you will experience in Heaven, even if all of this sounds too good to be true. Jesus paid dearly for this on your behalf.

On average, the thousands of people who have brought a single crime or hurt to the *Forgiving Path* experienced a

- 21% decrease in their desire to avoid the person who hurt them,
- 38% increase in feelings of empathy for them,
- 20% decrease in desire for revenge,
- 78% increase in the critical experience of justice for the crime.

That makes a noticeable difference. We never guilt participants into choosing to forgive. We merely show them how to access God's grace, power, and forgiveness for their situation.

In all our relationships, bad blood has shredded any possibility for true vulnerability and intimacy. There is a dark, foreboding shadow hovering over all interactions, emotional hair-triggers ready to erupt, and ever-present shame because we try and try but can't choose to forgive. Hear the good news—you can't forgive, but God-in-you can.

The following *Forgiveness Prayer* might help. It originated from a study of Matthew 18 and has helped many other couples.

"God, so how am I supposed to forgive my partner seventy times seven times? Right now, I don't want to. It's still not fair, or right, or just. What about me? My loss? My scars? I can't. I see that now. Now I get the heavenly joke. Unless I am regularly filled with Your DNA, by faith, through the Holy Spirit in my inner being, I will never be able to forgive the crime committed against me. Not even close. My cup does not have the capacity, and it leaks. Whether I want to admit it or not, I am far more like the wicked, boneheaded servant in Jesus' parable than the ever-full magnanimous King. I desperately

need You to make me feel the single absolute forgiveness that Jesus gained for me 2000 years ago. Then, make me want to forgive. Please give me some of your compassion, quick. Until that miracle occurs, I certainly am not free. Amen"

As you are doing this, Google the song "From Now On" by Flatirons Community Church one more time and let it pour over you.

P.S.: It has been the experience of thousands of people who have gone through the *Forgiving Path* that they find it easier to say they are sorry as well. It is intuitive, right? Let me ask you, why do you think that is?

QUESTIONS FOR PARTNERS TO CONSIDER

1. What did you hear that was new to you? Helpful? Explain.
2. When you heard the author say that you can't forgive, how did you feel? What was your knee-jerk reaction?
3. Are you the person who can't think of anything they need to forgive? Explore that thought a little deeper. Again, there is no judgment.

9

TIP #8: OKAY, YOU CAN BLAME GOD A LITTLE

(YOU'VE PROBABLY BEEN DOING THAT ALREADY)

"For even the very wise cannot see all ends...My heart tells me that [Gollum] has some part to play yet, for good or ill before the end"

— *GANDALF* IN *THE FELLOWSHIP OF THE RINGS*

ONE LAST ENCOURAGING thought for you and your relationship which we don't speak of enough.

I am a huge fan of the books by J.R.R. Tolkien and C.S. Lewis. They started writing young reader quest stories for the war-torn, decimated, PTSD'd British teens right after WWII. Their writing was remarkably powerful and hopeful, providing a sense of security for many and presenting a wonderful image of God's goodness and providence.

Though their young reader quest books never mention God, Jesus, or salvation, they evangelized an entire generation of teens. That is why I am currently writing similar modern fantasies for teen readers. They work.

If the two brilliant authors were sitting in your living room right now, considering your relational struggles, I believe they would be begging you to immerse yourself and your teens in 'good' quest stories. I am not kidding.

෨

PRE-COUCH EXERCISE:

Even if you've read them before, read Lewis' *The Chronicles of Narnia* quest series for young readers. Then add the *The Hobbit* and *The Lord of the Rings*.

෨

As I mentioned before, you are on a quest to find Father. I urge you to see this as an expanded quest, one that God himself ordained. You are called by the God of the universe, who loves you and your partner as much as the Father loves the Son and the Son loves the Father, to be in your current relationship. This is not by chance but by divine design.

Why? Because this is the very best path for you and your partner. I cannot provide specific proof. If this is a lesser path for either of you, God's love means nothing. Does that make sense?

With all the friction and difficulties, this may not be the quest you picked for yourself. I understand. Nevertheless, this was the holy quest God ordained for you and your partner. If there were a better choice, God would have provided an alternative. But he didn't. You are it.

What if you are remarried? That is above my pay grade, but you are on this journey now. It is good and right to see it as an opportunity to need God's love for your partner more each day. It is not a punishment. A bigger picture is at play. That does not mean your quest will be easy. Killing vicious dragons and conquering trolls and evil elves can be time-consuming and quite difficult. It simply means that God has picked you for this task. Why? Because no one else would do.

Pause, take a breath, and consider this: God chose you with your entire record of bad choices, history of less-than-perfect relationships, the many times you lacked faith, and times you said things to your partner you now regret and wish you could do-over. He chose you.

You didn't meet your partner by chance. I understand that in our 'sophisticated' post-Enlightenment West, we get nervous and uptight about the notion of God's providence, but that has been part of our problem. To us, when we think of providence, we imagine God interfering in our lives against our wills or stomping all over our free agency. I understand, but should we look at it slightly differently?

Please forgive me as I lead you through some nasty theological weeds. It will be worth it.

Let me illustrate from some passages from *The Fellowship of the Ring*. Gandalf, Frodo, and the rest of the fellowship are in the mines of Moriah. Frodo, who is already beginning to feel afraid that he is not the right person to carry the *One Ring*, notices that Gollum (whose real name is Smeagol) has been following them.

> Gandalf: *It's Gollum...He's been following us for three*
> *days...now the Ring has drawn him here, he will*
> *never be rid of his need for it, he hates and loves the*
> *Ring, as he hates and loves himself. Smeagol's life*
> *is a sad story. Yes, Smeagol he was once called*
> *before the Ring found him; before it drove*
> *him mad.*
>
> Frodo: *It's a pity Bilbo didn't kill him when he had*
> *the chance.*
>
> Gandalf: *Pity? It was pity that stayed Bilbo's hand.*
> *Many that live deserve death. Some that die*
> *deserve life. Can you give it to them Frodo? Do not*

be too eager to deal out death and judgment. Even the very wise cannot see all ends. My heart tells me that Gollum has some part to play yet, for good or ill before this is over. The pity of Bilbo may rule the fate of many.

Frodo: *I wish the ring had never come to me. I wish none of this had happened.*

Gandalf: *So do all who live to see such times. But that is not for them to decide. All we have to decide is what to do with the time that is given to us. There are other forces at work in this world Frodo, besides the will of evil. Bilbo was meant to find the Ring. In which case, you also were meant to have it. And that is an encouraging thought.*

Allow me some liberty here.

Partner: I wish I had never gotten together with my 'other.' It was a huge mistake. I am not the right person to carry this Ring.

Gandalf: Do not be too eager to deal out death and judgment to your relationship. Even the very wise cannot see all ends. My heart tells me that your partner has some part to play in your quest yet, for good or ill before this is over.

Partner: I wish the Ring had never come to me. I wish none of this had happened.

Gandalf: So do many who live to see such times. But that is not for them to decide. All we have to decide is what to do with the time that is given to us. There are other forces at work in this world, besides the will of evil. You were meant to find the Ring. In which case, you also were meant to have it. And that is an encouraging thought.

But what about my choice and free will? We enlightened Christians pit providence and free will against each other. Tolkien prefers a more layered view. Here's one person's thoughts on Tolkien's view of providence.

> *"Providence is the divine reason itself, the unfolding of temporal events as this is present to the vision of the divine mind; fate is this same unfolding of events as it is worked out in time, as we perceive it in the temporal world. We as human beings are unable to know providence; all we can know is fate...thus providence, which rules all things, also governs fate, which is the earthly manifestation of that rule... Whenever anything is done for one reason, but something other than what was intended happens on account of their reasons, it is called chance....but the chance occurred because the order which flows from providence, which disposes all things—even things unknown to men—brought the events together. Order and purpose, cause and effect always exist, but when man is ignorant of them, their results seem like chance."[1]*

Consider this. Every Christian knows that Jesus is 100% deity and 100% humanity, but no one can even come close to explaining that adequately. We are quite copacetic with accepting the 'both-and'

---

1. Dubs, Kathleen E. "Providence, Fate, and Chance: Boethian Philosophy in *The Lord of the Rings*." Tolkien and the Invention of Myth: A Reader. Ed. Jane Chance. Lexington: University Press of Kentucky, 2004. 135-6, quoted in Ivey, Christin (2008) "The Presence of Divine Providence in the Absence of "God": The Role of Providence, Fate, and Free Will in Tolkien Mythology," *The Corinthian*: Vol. 9, Article 2. Accessed Jan 9, 2025.

concept. I have embraced a similar perspective on providence and free will. They are both true and active, but they still seem, in my minuscule mind, to contradict each other. I find great comfort in a loving God who not only loves me but has also put me on a glorious quest, embracing all my predilections, foibles, and baggage. The quest's end is not up for grabs. It will accomplish everything He has divined, and I will share the joy of whatever accomplishments there will be. And yet, I have many choices to make. And my choices have consequences.

Here's Helen Lasseter.

"Gandalf is figuratively a messenger of providence to Middle-earth, urging other characters to act rightly out of hope. He reminds others of the hidden power—the unnamed force behind the scenes...In accord with his knowledge of providence, Gandalf guides and assists others in making right choices...While guiding all events and actions to an ultimate good, Providence never denies creatures their freedom...[Tolkien] shows that the person is integral to a providential world order; yet the person's inherent limitations, exposed through personal failure and defeat, reveal the constant presence of a higher and greater authority within the world."[2]

So, whether I have convinced you or not, don't you hope that I am right? Suffering and frustration are difficult enough, but to experience them with no greater purpose, accomplishing nothing in our lives, and being of no use to anyone is far worse.

Remember the biblical *quest* verse?

---

2. Lasseter, Helen T. "Fate, Providence, and Free Will: Clashing Perspectives of World Order in J.R.R. Tolkien's Middle-earth." Diss. Baylor University, 2006 (122, 164), quoted in Ivey, Christin (2008) "The Presence of Divine Providence in the Absence of "God": The Role of Providence, Fate, and Free Will in Tolkien Mythology," *The Corinthian*: Vol. 9, Article 2. Accessed Jan 9, 2025.

"And we know that in all things God works for the good of those who love him, who have been called according to his purpose." Rom 8:28

Your relationship, like a heroic character in a grand story, has been called for a specific, greater, and more valuable purpose divined by the stunning imagination of the heavenly director-producer God Himself because he cares for you and your spouse that much. It may not feel like it right now. Your quest will be challenging, difficult, and perhaps even maddening. But beloved, God's got this—and because of that, you will finish your God-given quest, and you will share glory unimaginable.

So, my guidance for you in this chapter is a bit unorthodox. Instead of reading the endless advice from the endless repetitive relationship books out there, please take a break and read *The Chronicles of Narnia, The Hobbit,* and *The Lord of the Rings.* If you prefer, enjoy watching Tolkien's masterpieces on video. They are excellent and will do nicely. Or check out my Kingdom Quest series (www.drbillsenyard.com) on Kindle and Amazon.

I hope to immerse your weary, battle-worn mind in enough epic quest stories that it begins—if only a little—to believe that your relationship might actually have a divine purpose, one that makes all the struggle worth it.

Tolkien's 'fairy tales,' which I refer to as 'quest tales,' also integrate the echo of the gospel in their plot, character development, and world-building. Such stories, according to Tolkien, are the most powerful and life-enhancing form of storytelling due to their unparalleled ability to reawaken a sense of wonder at the simple or ordinary things and for their capacity to empower anxious and insecure readers to escape the ugliness of the troubling and foreboding world around them.

According to Tolkien, creators of good tales are exercising their high God-given gift of 'sub-creation.' The telling and reading of such excellent stories cause us to experience our existential purposes. God created us to be people of good stories—hearing, creating and telling.

Tolkien writes,

> *"It is the mark of a good fairy story, of the higher or more complete kind, that however wild its events, however fantastic or terrible the adventures, it can give to child or man that hears it, when the 'turn' comes, a catch of the breath, a beat and lifting of the heart, near to (or indeed accompanied by) tears, as keen as that given by any form of literary art, and having a peculiar quality... Fantasy (in this sense) is, I think, not a lower but a higher form of Art, indeed the most nearly pure form, and so (when achieved) the most potent."*

Just for fun, read an excerpt from my own C.S. Lewis-esque, award-winning young reader's quest tale, *Tale of the Unlikely Prince*. Can you hear the shadows of a gospel presentation?

Young, insecure adolescent Prince Yeled is sent on a quest, no, a *great* quest, no, the greatest quest in the history of quests, to try to prove his worth and value to the King—and his mirror. He will need to learn that not all quests are alike, and this King is definitely not what he appears. He is sent out accompanied by the royal counselor, Noomai. However, the Prince ultimately proves to be an abysmal failure. Ashamed, he is on the long, arduous journey to face the King. Nomos, the Great King's royal vizier and mentor of Prince Yeled, meets him shortly before he returns to the castle and gives the lad something he did not expect.

(Nomos) "Tell me, lad, 'ow's the quest? Did you slay that nasty dragon?" Nomos asked, bringing up the elephant in the room.

"Nomos, with all due respect," opined Yeled. "I have failed badly. I have brought disgrace to myself and shame to my King. I am not worthy to be called his son."

Nomos paused for a while, not saying anything but compassionately gazing into the young lad's eyes. Then he spoke. "Oh, you foolish lad. Yer bum's oot the windae!" (Meaning: you're not making any sense.)

"Ah, lad, dinnae ya hear me. I didn't ask about those dragons. I could care less about those insignificant reptiles. I asked if you slayed the dragon. *That was your quest, you see." Nomos paused and rubbed his full beard thoughtfully. What he said next was very unexpected.*

"Boy, you dinnae hear the question right again. Will you tell me about your *dragon? Those other beasties come and go. I'm talking aboot the real dragon."*

The Royal Steward saw this as her cue and invited the confused Yeled to sit down on a nearby log.

"My prince," the steward gently added, "you are, whether you know it or not, even though you never asked for it; you are *a child of your father and mother. Inside your head is a hungry dragon voraciously consuming almost every compliment, every statement of love and every so-be'd honor. The beast quickly extinguishes any feelings of you being enough. Your dragon has been there for as long as you can remember and beyond, preventing you from feeling like the son any father would be proud of. So, the rest of your brain just kept working on feeding your beast. It's not all your fault. And so, your*

quest was ultimately designed for you to face that dragon—your dragon."

"I don't understand," exclaimed Yeled. "How can I slay a dragon I can't see? How can I slay a dragon that is in me? Is me?"

"Ya can't," said Nomos, interrupting as he placed one of his stubby fingers along the side of his nose to suggest, at last, the great secret was out. Nomos took out his long pipe. He had long given up smoking. It's bad for your health, you know. But it calmed him to put the unlit pipe in his mouth.

Then Nomos continued his thought. "That's the whole point—the irony of it all. Ya can't. You did all you could do, and it wasn't enough to even prick that dragon in ye. Now you have two paths left. You can keep feeding your inner dragon for the rest of your life. Good luck with that. You will never feel good enough. You will never feel your father is proud of you—enough."

"Or you can finally admit you can't do it and run helplessly to the arms of the King. There's real healing power there and there alone. Do what your parents wouldn't do—couldn't do. The choice is yours, lad."

"Irony again, ya left the presence of the King to find a putrid substitute for the presence of the King. But the further you went away, the worse ya felt. Simply put, the King knew ye would fail, humanly speaking. It was the goal of the quest, or at least the first level of the quest. Sometimes such shaming is a positive thing. In fact, redemptive shaming is a very good thing—or so I hear." He said the last part with a wink, a grin and a high jump where he clicked his heels.

"Even failure in the careful hands of a wise King can lead to an end far greater than all the successes of all time rolled into a single humongous ball. If, in yer failure, ye would come to see that ye are in greater need than ye have ever before imagined, it's all good. All ye ever needed was need, and ye dinnae have that until noo. And if the failure brings ya into his arms, what say ya?"

Nomos gave Yeled a toothy grin. He had practiced that line, and his delivery was flawless.

Do you hear the gospel? Does it offer you hope for your own delicate situation?

Here's Tolkien one last time. Imagine that he is not just speaking of his stories; he is also telling you something about your relationship.

> *"The consolation of fairy-stories, the joy of the happy ending: or more correctly of the good catastrophe, the sudden joyous "turn" (for there is no true end to any fairy-tale): this joy, which is one of the things which fairy-stories can produce supremely well, is not essentially "escapist," nor "fugitive." In its fairy-tale—or otherworld—setting, it is a sudden and miraculous grace: never to be counted on to recur. It does not deny the existence of dyscatastrophe, of sorrow and failure: the possibility of these is necessary to the joy of deliverance; it denies (in the face of much evidence, if you will) universal final defeat and in so far is evangelium, giving a fleeting glimpse of Joy, Joy beyond the walls of the world, poignant as grief."*
>
> — J.R.R. TOLKIEN, *TOLKIEN ON FAIRY STORIES*

In closing, Sam Gangee, Frodo's brave companion on his dangerous quest in *The Lord of the Rings*, was perhaps in your headspace. He realized that he just didn't want to finish his quest. It was way too hard, impossible really. Listen and be encouraged.

> *"We shouldn't be here at all, if we'd known more about it before we started. But I suppose it's often that way. The brave things in the old tales and songs, Mr. Frodo: adventures, as I used to call them. I used to think that they were things the wonderful folk of the stories went*

out and looked for, because they wanted them, because they were exciting and life was a bit dull, a kind of a sport, as you might say. But that's not the way of it with the tales that really mattered or the ones that stay in the mind. Folk seem to have been just landed in them, usually—their paths were laid that way, as you put it. But I expect they had lots of chances, like us, of turning back, only they didn't. And if they had, we shouldn't know, because they'd have been forgotten...I wonder what sort of a tale we've fallen into?...Don't the great tales never end?"

— J.R.R. TOLKIEN, *THE LORD OF THE RINGS*

Honored and beloved couple, you have been given a great tale to write, whether you wanted it or not.

At the end of your great quest, there will be a King who will run to you, embrace and kiss you, and exclaim, "You are my beloved child, with whom I am well pleased."

HOMEWORK:

- Watch the *The Fellowship of the Ring* (the first of *The Lord of the Rings* trilogy).[3] Now that you have read about Tolkien's faith, did *The Fellowship of the Ring* feel different to you? Does this change how you see your relationship a little? Please unpack this.
- Google "Jireh" by Elevation Worship and Maverick City Music (2021) and just let it pour over you.

---

3. Jackson, P. (Director) (2001). The Lord of the Rings: The Fellowship of the Ring [Film; four-disc special extended ed on DVD]. WingNut Films; The Saul Zaentz Company

QUESTIONS FOR PARTNERS TO CONSIDER

1. What did you hear that was new to you? Helpful?
2. What kind of counseling is this?
3. Did you know that reading a good book can lower your anxiety level by 68%? And it's cheaper than most drugs. Thoughts?

10

TIP #9: DEFINE YOURSELF RADICALLY AS ONE BELOVED BY GOD

"Define yourself radically as one beloved by God. This is the true self. Every other identity is illusion."

— BRENNAN MANNING

IN CLOSING, I want to remind you of the nine, Pre-Couch, simple and surprising tips:

- Tip #1: Stop It!
- Tip #2: Your Relationship Is Only Mostly Dead
- Tip #3: You Can't Do It
- Tip #4: Feeling Lonely is Not All Your Partner's Fault
- Tip #5: The Reason You Feel Stuck and Powerless is You Are
- Tip #6: You Have Daddy Issues
- Tip #7: You Were Right All Along, You Can't Forgive
- Tip #8: Okay, You Can Blame God a Little
- Tip #9: Define Yourself Radically as One Beloved by God

Couples, how do you feel after reading *Before the Couch*? I hope you have gleaned some ideas, hope, and encouragement from this book. The last thing I ever wanted to do was to add to your burden. Relationships are indeed complicated and hard. Broken relationships are even more complex. However, remember that you're not alone in this struggle. All relationships are broken. Amen? Let's see what we accomplished.

- I promised not to shame or guilt you—Check
- I promised to keep the tips simple and surprising —Check
- I promised to toss in humor now and then—Check
- I said at the very beginning, stop doing what you are doing. It's obviously not working, and I developed it further in every chapter. God loves misfits with all the love in the Universe. You haven't messed that up. You can't—Check
- I asked you to watch *The Chosen*, read a young reader's fantasy series, listen to some great music, pray a few provocative prayers, accused you of having daddy issues, and explained that one of the reasons you are struggling is God Himself has ordained a heroic quest for you—one that requires you to fail so you will finally trust Him —Check.

Well, how are you doing? Are you feeling a little better about your relationship now? About yourself? About God? Have you noticed some movement? Have you felt a little hope?

In closing, hear the wonderful Brennan Manning.

"When I get honest, I admit I am a bundle of paradoxes. I believe and I doubt, I hope and get discouraged, I love and I hate, I feel bad about feeling good, I feel guilty about not feeling guilty. I am trusting and suspicious. I am honest and I still play games. Aristotle said I am a rational animal; I say I am an angel with an incredible capacity for beer. To live by grace means to acknowledge my whole life story, the light side and the dark. In admitting my shadow side, I learn who I am and what God's grace means. As Thomas Merton put it, 'A saint is not someone who is good but who experiences the goodness of God.' The gospel of grace nullifies our adulation of televangelists, charismatic superstars, and local church heroes. It obliterates the two-class citizenship theory operative in many American churches. For grace proclaims the awesome truth that all is gift. All that is good is ours not by right but by the sheer bounty of a gracious God. While there is much we may have earned--our degree and our salary, our home and garden, a Miller Lite and a good night's sleep--all this is possible only because we have been given so much: life itself, eyes to see and hands to touch, a mind to shape ideas, and a heart to beat with love. We have been given God in our souls and Christ in our flesh. We have the power to believe where others deny, to hope where others despair, to love where others hurt. This and so much more is sheer gift; it is not reward for our faithfulness, our generous disposition, or our heroic life of prayer. Even our fidelity is a gift, 'If we but turn to God,' said St. Augustine, 'that itself is a gift of God.' My deepest awareness of myself is that I am deeply loved by Jesus Christ, and I have done nothing to earn it or deserve it."

FOUR *BEFORE THE COUCH* PRAYERS AND GOSPEL MESSAGES

Here are the prayers and Gospel messages highlighted in the book. Now you don't have to track them down as you say them twice a day for as long as it takes for you to notice a difference. There are a lot of things that we have pointed out that you just *can't* do. You *can* say these aloud.

THE SIMPLE UNCLUTTERED GOSPEL (CHAPTERS 3 & 6)

"Jesus-Follower, strictly because of what Jesus did for you 2000 years ago, God actually loves you. He loves you with all His heart, as much as the Father loves the Son and the Son loves the Father. He can't love you any more or any less than He does right now—even if you were a better partner. He loves you as you are, not as you should be or could be. You can't add to this love or take away from it. Now I get it, it often feels like you've messed it up, or need to do something so God would like you better. Not so. How do you experience it more now? Simple! Good news, there is something you can do and are invited to do. You can take daily baby steps to ask the Spirit inside of you to make you know, experience, and feel just how much God loves you right now. Just ask. Ask again later today. Ask tomorrow. Make it a spiritual habit."

THE MAKE ME PRAYER (CHAPTER 4)

(part 1)

"God, right now I am hurting, depressed, angry, feeling disrespected, unloved, hopeless, beat-up, feeling ashamed and like a failure...and that's just the tip of the iceberg. I really don't like this person. I wish I

had never known them. To some degree, I despise them. I am also afraid of them. I can't take it being with them, being near them anymore. My body has a visceral reaction when I am in the same room. Honestly, I am at the end of my rope. I admit that You love them as they are, even after all the things they did to me and the many things they didn't do for me. I don't. I confess I am way out of sync with You. This frightens me. Honestly, I am afraid You <u>can</u> make me love them again. I am not sure at all that I want that to happen. I am done. However, I <u>am</u> willing to come to You to ask that You make me feel loved by You again. I need that. I want that desperately. Holy Spirit, unleash Your faith in my inner being and make love happen for me. Now, please. Amen."

(part 2- when you are ready)

Holy Spirit, I am also begging that You give me Your love for them. This is hard right now. I am not sure I really want it. This is scary. So, give me Your perfect love that casts out fears. Give me wisdom so I don't do something foolish. Amen.

THE QAYEEN PRAYER (CHAPTER 7)

"God, I am beginning to see I am afraid of trusting You. Trusting has not been good for me—betrayal, broken trust—all too painful. In my head, I want to look up and see into Your eyes. Yet I am scared to death of what I may see. I can't. I won't. I need Your power to enable me to look up—to want to look up. To be honest, I wonder if You would ever say to me, 'This is my beloved son or daughter, with whom I am well pleased.' I want to hear You say it. I want to believe it is true. In my brain, I know Jesus purchased it for me. I have a hard time believing it in my soul. I desperately want to hear You say

it to me. Make me believe it is so. I need to feel the honor of being a child of Yours in good standing. I have endured great dishonor and disrespect here. Make me receive the honor of adoption that Jesus paid so dearly for. Now, please. I am weary of all the games I am playing. I am tired of being lonely, being afraid, blaming You, my partner, myself, and others, wearing masks, acting out, and holding up boundaries to protect my heart. Spirit, quick, give me power to look up and experience Father."

FORGIVENESS PRAYER (CHAPTER 8)

"God, so how am I supposed to forgive my partner seventy times seven times? Right now, I don't want to. It's still not fair, or right, or just. What about me? My loss? My scars? I can't. I see that now. Now I get the heavenly joke. Unless I am regularly filled with Your DNA, by faith, through the Holy Spirit in my inner being, I will never be able to forgive the crime committed against me. Not even close. My cup does not have the capacity, and it leaks. Whether I want to admit it or not, I am far more like the wicked, boneheaded servant in Jesus' parable than the ever-full magnanimous King. I desperately need You to make me feel the single absolute forgiveness that Jesus gained for me 2000 years ago. Then, make me want to forgive. Please give me some of your compassion, quick. Until that miracle occurs, I certainly am not free. Amen"

Couples, you've got this. Be encouraged.

The End.

THANKS SO MUCH!

Couples, if *Before the Couch* has benefited your marriage, we'd greatly appreciate your support with a review on Amazon.

Simply use the QR code below, then scroll down to *"Write a Customer Review"* near the bottom of the page. Your feedback will help us reach other couples who need this message.

Thank you in advance for your support!

www.ingramcontent.com/pod-product-compliance
Lightning Source LLC
Chambersburg PA
CBHW071319130626
46556CB00004B/1665